Lecture Notes in Computer Science   9980

Commenced Publication in 1973
Founding and Former Series Editors:
Gerhard Goos, Juris Hartmanis, and Jan van Leeuwen

More information about this series at http://www.springer.com/series/7408

Vicenç Torra

Scala: From a Functional Programming Perspective

An Introduction to the Programming Language

Vicenç Torra
University of Skövde
Skovde
Sweden

ISSN 0302-9743 ISSN 1611-3349 (electronic)
Lecture Notes in Computer Science
ISBN 978-3-319-46480-0 ISBN 978-3-319-46481-7 (eBook)
DOI 10.1007/978-3-319-46481-7

Library of Congress Control Number: 2016952527

LNCS Sublibrary: SL2 – Programming and Software Engineering

Printed on acid-free paper

This Springer imprint is published by Springer Nature
The registered company is Springer International Publishing AG
The registered company address is: Gewerbestrasse 11, 6330 Cham, Switzerland

To my mother and grandmother

Una tarde parda y fría
de invierno. Los colegiales
estudian. Monotonía
de lluvia tras los cristales.
(Antonio Machado)

Que jo mateixa, si no fos tan llega,
en lletra clara contaria el fet
(Pere Quart, Bestiari)

Preface

I started learning functional programming with LISP, and then I learnt Standard ML. I used LISP for several years as my programming language for research, exploiting its functional programming characteristics, and Standard ML for teaching functional programming. This greatly influenced the way I program.

Programming languages are a matter of taste. I like functional programming, recursivity, and immutable objects. I think that this makes programming simpler and fun. In addition, I like LISP for its syntactic simplicity, both for programming and for structuring data. I used LISP regularly in the past, and although I am not using it regularly now, I still use it when I need to make a simple program quickly. I also consider Standard ML a nice language. I like its conciseness, its type inference system, and that it is simple to define algebraic data types.

Later I met other functional programming languages. Haskell, with lazy evaluation and lazy lists, and Scheme, with its continuations.

I have included in my personal list of programming languages Scala, which integrates functional programming into the object-oriented paradigm. It also permits the use of functional programming constructions in the context of big data, with its integration with Spark. In addition, it includes actors as one of its parallel mechanisms. Actors are a high level model that integrates well with object-oriented programming.

This book is an introduction to Scala from this functional programming perspective. The origin of this book is in the notes of a course on *Advanced Programming* we started in 2015–2016 at the University of Skövde. The course belongs to the Master on Data Science and focuses on functional programming using Scala.

I see Scala as an object-oriented programming language that supports rather effectively functional programming. This introduction presents Scala, focusing on this functional programming part. Nevertheless, in order to make concepts clear, and because it is a crucial part of the language, I also include some description of the object-oriented aspect of Scala.

This focus makes me ignore or give less importance to some other characteristics of the language. All programmers know that some problems can be solved from different perspectives. For example, we can define stacks (or lists) by means of an algebraic data type, but also by means of linked cells in memory with pointers. The former follows a functional programming style while the latter a more imperative style. In this book, stressing functional programming, I focus on the definition of abstract data types, recursion, and the like. Less importance is given to variables and to iteration. For a more imperative approach, [9] is a nice alternative.

In the same way, functions are first declared by means of val, and our discussion on method declaration def is deferred to a latter section. This differs from other books as e.g., [3], (a book that presents Scala as a functional language). For Scala from the object-oriented paradigm, you can consider [8].

The book is by no means a complete description of the language. That is, it does not provide information on all constructions and functions of the language. The Internet offers enough material on line for this. So, I have not written the book with this purpose. Its goal is to provide an introduction (a concise one) of the language from this functional programming perspective. Nevertheless, I believe that the book is self-contained and contains enough material to enable readers to use it to learn the language and eventually use it also as a reference. An index is included for this purpose.

In addition, this text having been prepared for a course on advanced programming and for master students, I discuss and compare Scala's approach with those of other languages. I think that it is good for any programmer, and naturally for any computer engineer, to know different languages and ways to tackle programming problems. It is well known that while some languages are better in some aspects, they are not the simplest for all purposes. In the book, I mention and compare Scala with e.g., Java, Standard ML (SML), and Prolog. The most detailed comparison is in the chapter devoted to algebraic data types. I consider that SML offers a simpler way to define them and this is explained in the text in some detail.

Organization of the Book

The book is divided into eight chapters. The first one is an introduction to functional programming, its main characteristics and languages. The second one presents the basics of the Scala language. The most important concepts seen there are the functions. We also give an overview of lists as well as other types of sequences. We introduce pattern matching. Chapter 3 presents lazy evaluation, which permits us to define infinite lists. At this point we introduce (Chapter 4) the main concepts and definitions related to Scala as an object-oriented programming language. We show how to define classes and methods. We also see traits and packages. Chapter 5 focuses on classes with polymorphic types. Functional programming tries to define functions as generally as possible. Because of that, polymorphism plays an important role. Chapter 6 focuses again on object-oriented aspects. The chapter explains how the object-oriented and the functional elements in Scala interact. We discuss tail-recursive functions that permit an efficient implementation (compilation) of recursive functions into an imperative language. Chapter 7 is devoted to algebraic data types. These types are characteristic of functional programming languages. We explain how to define them in Scala. We also compare their definition with the one offered by Standard ML. The book finishes in Chapter 8 with parallelism in Scala. We focus on two models: parallel collections and actors.

How to Use This book

We expect readers to be programmers using imperative/object-oriented languages. Knowledge of functional programming is not a prerequisite.

As I explained above, this book has been used in our course on advanced programming at the University of Skövde. The content has been used in 10 sessions of 2 hours each. We explained the main concepts (except Chapter 8) and did most of the exercises.

The book has been prepared with examples, exercises, and solutions to permit self-study. We have a web page for this book available under the following URL: http://www.mdai.cat/scala.

Programming and programming languages can only be learnt by doing. Therefore it is expected that readers install the language, test the examples, and program themselves in Scala.

Acknowledgments

My first acknowledgment goes to Ulises Cortés, who introduced me to the functional programming paradigm with the LISP programming language around 1990. Then, to the SAIL research group at the University of Skövde, in which I am integrated and which launched the Master on Data Science where this material has been used. Special thanks go to Elio Ventocilla, who read this material in its previous version and gave me useful comments. Last and not least, to the students of the master that used the first version of this material while I was producing it. All errors are, of course, my own.

August 2016   Vicenç Torra

Contents

Chapter 1
An Introduction to Functional Programming Languages

Functional programming is a programming paradigm that has one of its roots in the programming language LISP. LISP, which stands for *LISt Processing*, was created in 1958 by John McCarthy. Its main characteristic is that computation is in terms of functions and recursion. Syntaxis in LISP is based on the use of a prefix notation and the parenthesis, no much syntactic sugar is used. For example, the function to compute the factorial can be written as follows in LISP:

```
(defun factorial (n) (if (= n 0) 1 (* n (factorial (- n 1)))))
```

The theoretical basis of functional programming is λ-calculus, developed by A. Church in the 30s. The development of λ-calculus was parallel (or a little earlier [16, 29]) to the development of Turing machines by A. Turing. Both were developed as computational models and were proven equivalent from the point of view of the functions they can compute. They were independently used to prove the *Entscheidungsprobleme*[1] (decision problem). While Turing machines rely on the concept of state and transition functions between states, λ-calculus relies on the concept of rewriting.

Functional programming sees programs as functions, and functions are decomposed into other functions. In pure functional programming the only value that the function computes is what it returns, there are not side effects, and the input values are not modified.

For example, a typical implementation of the factorial in an imperative language is as follows.

```
function factorial (var n: integer) return integer is
   result := 1;
   for i=1 to n loop
     result := result*i;
```

---

[1] Entscheidungsproblem is one of Hilbert's mathematical problems.

© Springer International Publishing AG 2016
V. Torra, *Scala: From a Functional Programming Perspective*, LNCS 9980
DOI: 10.1007/978-3-319-46481-7_1

```
   end for
   return (result);
end function
```

Observe that variables i and result change their values while the loop is executed. Compare that with the variable n in the recursive definition of factorial. Note that the value n does not change.

So, a main difference between functional programming and imperative programming is that in the latter, programming is achieved by means of a modification of the variables in the program. This corresponds to changing the states, as in the Turing machine.

1.1   Main Characteristics of Functional Programming Languages

We have underlined above that functional programming has as its main characteristic in that programs are based on the definition of functions. Functions are the main elements in programs. The main properties of functional programming languages include the following (we include the section were these concepts are studied).

- Expressions without side effects (Sect. 2.6.4)
- First-class functions (Sect. 2.6). This includes

  - Pass functions as arguments
  - Return functions
  - Assign them to variables and to data structures
  - Anonymous functions

- Higher-order functions (Sect. 2.6.5)
- Recursion (Sect. 2.6.7)
- Immutable data structures (Sect. 2.9.1)
- Lazy evaluation (Chap. 3)
- Do not require tail-recursive optimization (Sect. 6.1)

This compares with the main characteristics of imperative programming languages.

- Commands are the main components of the language
- Functions and procedures
- Iteration and loops
- Mutable objects
- Eager evaluation
- Recursion is not supported

Table 1.1 compares functional programming and imperative programming. The table also includes the logic programming paradigm.

Table 1.1 Differences between the functional, logic and imperative paradigms.

	Functional	Logic	Imperative
A program as a	Function	Relationship	Command
Building blocks	Expressions (evaluation)	Horn clauses (true/false?)	Assignment (execution)
Program Construction	Composing functions	Defining facts and rules	Sequences of commands
Variables	Immutable (let x be)	Immutable (let x be)	Mutable (memory cell)
Repetition	Recursion	Recursion	Loop

1.2 Some Functional Programming Languages

In this section we review briefly four functional languages that have had a strong influence in the development of this type of languages. The list of functional programming languages is, however, very large and includes e.g. Miranda, Hope, and Erlang.

1.2.1 LISP

This is the classical functional programming language. It was created by J. McCarthy 1958 and described in [12]. See [13] for details on its creation. It received influence from the Information Processing Language (a language created between 1955 and 1956), which already implemented concepts as recursion and list-processing. This language is still alive and used today and has influenced indirectly most functional programming languages and directly the language Scheme.

1.2.2 FP

This language was proposed by J. Backus and it is a kind of *Extreme Functional Programming* language, with no variables. The internal product IP of two vectors is defined as follows.

Def IP $\equiv$ /+ o α x o trans

Here, Trans is the transpose of the two vectors of the input (seen as a matrix). Then, we apply the product to all pairs of numbers and finally we add them[2].

Another example is the product of two matrices. Their definition is as follows.

Def MM $\equiv$ (α α IP) o (α distl) o distr o [1, trans o 2]

---

[2]This definition is similar to the solution of Exercise 2.8, the internal product in Scala. In this case, Trans is translated to Scala in `zip`, α x corresponds to a map of the product, and /+ that extends the addition for a pair of numbers to a sequence can be translated to Scala by fold.

The language FP is described by Backus (well known for the development of the language FORTRAN and the BNF - Backus-Naur form) in [2]. Dijkstra presented in 1979 (see [5]) a critic of the paper by Backus [2].

1.2.3 Standard ML (SML)

This is a strongly (statically) typed functional programming language. This language is able to deduce the type of objects and functions. SML permits to define algebraic data types easily. This is discussed in Sect. 7.1 (examples in SML will be given).

1.2.4 Haskell

One of its main characteristics is that includes lazy evaluation, which made it more popular. For example, Standard ML did not include lazy evaluation, but most languages since Haskell include it. We will see lazy evaluation in Sect. 3.

1.3 Scala

Scala was created by Martin Odersky. It combines the features of functional programming languages and object oriented programming. I would say that it is an object oriented programming that incorporates functional programming concepts and paradigms. It is implemented using the Java programming language and its virtual machine (JVM). Because of that, some of the types, classes, and methods in Java are available when we program in Scala.

1.4 Running Scala

The language can be installed from the official language webpage:
http://www.scala-lang.org

The language can be used as an interpreted language. In this case, you need to call scala from the computer prompt. With this command, you start the interpreter and can begin your programming. For example, you can test it by printing "Hello, World!" and doing the operations 2+2 and -5. In this case you will get something similar to the following.

```
computer@user ~
$ scala
Welcome to Scala version 2.11.6
                    (Java HotSpot(TM) Client VM, Java 1.8.0_45).
Type in expressions to have them evaluated.
Type :help for more information.

scala> println("Hello, World!")
Hello, World!

scala> 2+2
res1: Int = 4

scala> -5
res2: Int = -5
```

The term REPL for Read-Execute-Print Loop corresponds to the execution of the interpreter in this way. That is, the interpreter reads a definition, executes it and prints the result.

We can also load (text) files with commands and definitions into the interpreter. Let us edit the (text) file MyFirstFile.scala and write the following text.

```
println("Hello, World!")
2+2
-2
```

We can load this file in the interpreter using

```
:load MyFirstFile.scala
```

The file is interpreted by the interpreter (REPL) and we obtain the following results on the screen.

```
scala> :load MyFirstFile.scala
Loading MyFirstFile.scala...
Hello, World!
res1: Int = 4
res2: Int = -2
```

The file can naturally include more elaborate definitions and computations.

An alternative is to write the programs in files, compile them and then execute the resulting compiled file. Scala programs are compiled for the Java Virtual Machine. Let us illustrate this approach editing a file with name MyFirstProgram.scala that includes the following definition.

```
object MyFirstProgram {
  def main (args: Array[String]): Unit = {
    println("Hello, World!")
  }
}
```

This text defines an object called `MyFirstProgram` with a method called main that prints `"Hello, World!"`. Details on the definition of an object in this way can be found in Sect. 4.6. At this point notice that instead of the `println` command we can include other expressions and definitions.

We can compile this file with the command `scalac` and then execute it with the command `scala`. In this way we execute the method `main` of the object `MyFirstProgram`.

```
computer@user ~
$ scalac MyFirstProgram.scala

computer@user ~
$ scala MyFirstProgram.scala
Hello, World!
```

Scala documentation gives guidelines for the content of a file. They are the following.

> As a rule, files should contain a single logical compilation unit. By logical I mean a class, trait or object. One exception to this guideline is for classes or traits which have companion objects. Companion objects should be grouped with their corresponding class or trait in the same file. These files should be named according to the class, trait or object they contain (Scala documentation, Style guide, Files [23])

In addition, we can also use an Integrated Development Environment (IDE), as ECLIPSE / ScalaIDE [27], for programming in Scala, or tools like Jupyter Notebook [26].

Chapter 2
The Basics of the Language

*Ordo autem qui in verbis attenditur est
illud per quod verba tam in loquente
quam in audientibus virtutem et
efficaciam sortiuntur.*
Ramon Llull, Rethorica nova [VII].

In this chapter we give a quick review of the most basic elements of the language. We begin reviewing the data types that the language provides by default. Then, we review the syntaxis for statements and declarations (e.g. conditional and loops). We also discuss definition of functions, higher-order functions and the use of pattern recognition in functions. Our discussion on functions include also recursion. The chapter includes also definitions of lists and other types of collections predefined in Scala which can be naturally processed using recursive functions.

2.1 Data Types

Java provides the usual types that implement integers, and real numbers, Boolean and characters. They are the basic types. Class names and precisions of the basic data types in Scala are given in Table 2.1. Usual functions are defined for objects in these classes.

Scala and Java. As explained above, Scala is based on Java. That is why we have in Scala the same types we have in Java with the same precision. Nevertheless, there are some differences due to a different structure in the system of classes. In Java, the primitive data types (byte, short, int, long, char, float, double and boolean) are not classes, and, thus, do not belong to the hierarchy of objects. In addition to these primitive data types, Java have the classes as e.g. Integer, Long which have some methods implemented. In Scala there is no such distinction. These types are classes, and methods are directly implemented on the classes. Therefore, there is also a difference on how some methods are called/applied in Scala and Java.

© Springer International Publishing AG 2016
V. Torra, *Scala: From a Functional Programming Perspective*, LNCS 9980
DOI: 10.1007/978-3-319-46481-7_2

Table 2.1 Basic data types in Scala: Type names and precision. Byte, Short, Int, Long, Float, Double and Char are numeric types. All of them are signed except Char that is an unsigned integer. Boolean and Unit are non-numeric types. For details on the actual implementation see Scala documentation.

Type name	Precision
Byte	8 bit signed integer. [Byte.MinValue=−128, Byte.MaxValue=127]
Short	16 bit signed integer. [Short.MinValue=−32768, Short.MaxValue=32767]
Int	32 bit signed integer. [−2147483648, 2147483647]
Long	64 bit signed integer. [−9223372036854775808, 9223372036854775807]
Float	32 bit IEEE-754 floating point number
Double	64 bit IEEE-754 floating point number
Char	16 bit unsigned integer (Unicode char). Range [U+0000,U+FFFF]
Boolean	Values true and false
Unit	There is only one value of type Unit ()

The classes of these types are `value classes`. `Value classes` are a particular type of classes that are implemented in a more efficient way. Details on value classes as well as an explanation on how to define new ones are given in Sect. 4.3. At this point, the fact of being value classes or not is not relevant.

We review below some of the basic operations defined for basic data types.

- **Value class Int.** Usual operations are implemented in Scala. For example, the following ones.

  – Arithmetic. Addition (+), subtraction (−), product (*), quotient (/), reminder (%)
  – Comparison (`<`, `>`, `==`, `<=`, `>=`, `!=`), shifts (`>>`, `<<`), bitwise operations (`|` for OR, `&` for AND, `^` for XOR), absolute value (abs as e.g. `x.abs` for an integer value x), maximum (`x.max`), minimum (`x.min`).
  – Transformation to `String`. + (binary operator with a string in its first argument).

  Examples of valid expressions:

  ```
  2+2         3<4          5>=6
  2|10        1|10         3|11
  3.abs       1.max(3)     3.min(5)
  ```

- **Value class Double.** Similar operations exist for Double (including reminder). In addition we have the following (functionality is as expected):

  – `floor`, `ceil`, `isInfinite()`, `isNan()`

- **Value class Boolean.**

  – Comparison (`==`).
  – Logical connectives. And (`&`, `&&`), or (`|`, `||`), xor (`^`), negation (`!`, this operator is prefix so used as `!true`). `&` and `|` evaluate the two arguments (eager evaluation). `&&` and `||` do not necessarily evaluate both (i.e., they use lazy evaluation).

Scala Language Specification (Version 2.11): Section 6.12.1. Prefix operations

A prefix operation $op; e$ consists of a prefix operator op, which must be one of the identifiers $+$, $-$, $!$ or . The expression $op; e$ is equivalent to the postfix method application e.unary_op.

Prefix operators are different from normal function applications in that their operand expression need not be atomic. For instance, the input sequence $-\sin(x)$ is read as $-(\sin(x))$, whereas the function application negate $\sin(x)$ would be parsed as the application of the infix operator sin to the operands negate and (x).

Fig. 2.1 Prefix operators in Scala according to Scala Language Specification (Version 2.11).

For a discussion of prefix and infix operators, and on precedence of operators see Figs. 2.1 and 2.2.

Prefix and infix. We have an infix operator when it goes between its arguments. In mathematics, addition and substraction are usually expressed by the infix operators $+$ and $-$ as e.g. in $2 + 2$ and $2 - 1$. We have a prefix operator when it goes before the arguments. The expression -2 has a prefix operator $-$.

It is usual to mix prefix and infix operators, but there are languages where all operations are prefix. This is the case of LISP where we have the name of the function always first. So, an expression as $2 + 3 * 3 + sqrt(5 + 4)$ is expressed in LISP as follows:

```
(+ 2 (* 3 3) (sqrt (+ 5 4)))
```

2.1.1 Strings

Among the predefined types of Scala we find Strings. They are defined as in most languages by double quotes. We can determine the length of a string (with `length`), concatenate them (with `concat` and with +), compare them (with ==), and select the element at a given position (with `charAt(position)`). Other methods from `java.lang.String` can also be used in Scala (e.g., `toUpperCase`, and `compareToIgnoreCase`). So, the following are valid operations with strings:

```
"a, b, c; alpha beta gamma; 1, 2, and 3"
"one" + "two" + "three"
"one".concat("two") == "one" + "two"
"one".compareToIgnoreCase("ONE")
"one".charAt(0)+"one".charAt(1)+"one".charAt(2)
```

Note that the last expression returns 322 because `charAt` returns a char that is a 16 bit unsigned integer (Unicode char)! Also note that the initial character of a string is at position zero.

Scala Language Specification (Version 2.11): 6.12.3 Infix operations
An infix operator can be an arbitrary identifier. Infix operators have precedence
and associativity defined as follows:
The *precedence* of an infix operator is determined by the operator's first character.
Characters are listed below in increasing order of precedence, with characters on
the same line having the same precedence.

```
(all letters)
|
^
&
= !
< >
:
+ -
* / \%
(all other special characters)
```

That is, operators starting with a letter have lowest precedence, followed by
operators starting with |, etc.
There's one exception to this rule, which concerns *assignment operators*. The
precedence of an assignment operator is the same as the one of simple assignment
(=). That is, it is lower than the precedence of any other operator.
The *associativity* of an operator is determined by the operator's last character.
Operators ending in a colon ':' are right-associative. All other operators are
left-associative.

Fig. 2.2 Infix operators in Scala according to Scala Language Specification (Version 2.11).

It is important to know that strings are immutable[1] objects.

Scala includes three types of interpolators for strings. Interpolators permit us
to include in a string expressions that need to be evaluated (e.g. variables to be
replaced by their value). The three types are s, t, and raw interpolation. s permits
to evaluate expressions, t is similar to printf in the C language, and raw does
not scape the \ characters. We do not go into details of this, but just consider the
following examples that permit to replace an expression by its computation, and
prints \n without replacing it by a new line.

```
println(s"The maximum between 1 and 8 is ${1.max(8)}")
println(raw"\n 1 \n 2 \n 3")
```

The output in Scala is as follows..

```
scala> println(s"The maximum between 1 and 8 is ${1.max(8)}")
The maximum between 1 and 8 is 8

scala> println(raw"\n 1 \n 2 \n 3")
\n 1 \n 2 \n 3
```

---

[1]Immutable objects are discussed in Sect. 2.9.1

2.2 Statements and Expressions

We review in this section some of the basic constructions in Scala.

- Conditional. It is similar to conditional in most languages. We have the following

```
if(BooleanExpression) { Expression }
```

```
if(BooleanExpression) { ExpressionTrue }
   else { ExpressionFalse }
```

  We use here expressions for the then and the else branches. In fact, being Scala an object oriented language, we can use commands (and sequences of commands) in both then and else branches. When we have single expressions, we can remove the curly brackets.
- Loops. As we focus on functional programming, we will avoid loops as much as possible in our programs. Nevertheless, they are explained here for the sake of completeness. We have while and do-while loops that can be used as follows.

```
while (BooleanExpression) { Expression }
```

```
do { Expression } while (BooleanExpression)
```

  There are also for loops in Scala. We will discuss them later in Sect. 2.9.3, but for the time being, they can be used as in the following example.

```
for (i <- 1 to 10) { statement }
```

  Then, we will execute the statement ten times and the variable i will take values 1, 2, 3, …, 10, as expected, in the 10 consecutive executions of the statement.

2.3 Statement Separator and Blocks

Newline separates statements in Scala. Alternatively we can use semicolon ";" to separate statements, when needed. Published code usually do not have much semicolons. So, the code

```
statement1
statement2
```

is equivalent to the following:

```
statement1; statement2
```

Blocks of statements use curly brackets. For example,

```
{ statement; statement }
```

2.4 Comments

We can include comments in the following two ways.

```
/* Multiple
   line
   comment */
```

```
// One line comment
```

2.5 Declarations

We can associate values to identifiers using val and var. We use them as follows

```
val nameConstant: Type = expression
var nameVariable: Type = expression
```

With val we are defining a constant, and we associate it with a value. This association can no longer be changed. With var we are defining a variable (in an imperative sense) and associate it to a value that can be later changed. We will revisit the difference between both val and var in Sect. 2.9 when discussing mutable and immutable data structures.

To change the value of a variable defined with var, we just assign another value to it. Observe the following.

```
val a1 = 2*5
var a3 = 4*6
a3 = 8484
```

In the interpreter, constants defined with val can be redeclared, but they cannot be really overwritten. Observe the following.

```
scala> val a1 = 2*5
a1: Int = 10
scala> a1 = 54
<console>:8: error: reassignment to val
       a1 = 54
          ^

scala> val a1 = 54
a1: Int = 54
```

Note that a1 cannot be redefined, but we can declare the same name again. This is, in fact, as defining a new constant which can be seen as hiding the scope of the previous definition.

Declarations in functional programming. We will mainly use in this text `val` because we understand variables in a mathematical way (as in mathematical expressions *Let X be ...*). That is, as constants that do not change their values. We do not see them as positions of memory whose value can be changed.

2.5.1 Composite Types: Cartesian Products

We can use basic types and compose them. We can also define variables as the cartesian product of two or more types. For example, the following is a valid declaration in Scala.

```
val a1 = (2*5,"ten")
```

We can access the elements of the products by means of `._1`, `._2`, etc. So, `a1._1` will return 10.

2.5.2 Nested Declarations

We can include declarations inside other declarations. That is, nested declarations are possible in Scala. This can help on the calculation of a value. Note that the declarations inside another declarations are not accessible from outside.

In the following example, `a1` and `a2` are local to the definition of a.

```
val a = {
  val a1 = 10
  val a2 = "In text:"+a1+"is ten"
  (a1, a2)
  }
```

Check that the values of `a1` and `a2` are not available once the declaration of a is completed. So, the scope of `a1` and `a2` is only within a.

2.6 Functions

The declaration of a function can be done by means of code with the following structure: list of arguments between parenthesis, the symbol "=>", and the body of the function. The following are simple examples of functions.

```
(a:Int)  =>  2*a
(a:Int,  b:Int)  =>  a+b
(a:Int,  f:Int=>Int)  =>  f(a)
```

The first function has a single integer parameter (with name a and type Int) and multiplies it by two. The second function has two integer parameters (with names a and b and types Int) and adds them.

The third function has two parameters. The first parameter is an integer (parameter a) and the second one is a function (parameter f) that given an integer computes another integer. The body of the third function shows that applies f to a. Note that the type of the parameter a is Int. The type of the function f is Int => Int because it receives an Int and returns => another Int.

In general, the type of a function with n arguments has the following structure.

```
Type1,  Type2,  ...,  TypeN => OutputType
```

The functions we have seen are anonymous. That is, they have no name. Nevertheless, they can be applied and passed to other functions. For example, we can apply the first function to 3 as follows:

```
((a:Int)=>2*a)(3)
```

and we can pass the first anonymous function to the third anonymous functions as follows (together with the integer 3 as the latter needs two parameters. This is done as follows.

```
((a:Int,  f:Int=>Int)  =>  f(a))(3,((a:Int)=>2*a))
```

Exercise 2.1. Given the three parameters of a 2nd degree equation

$$ax^2 + bx + c = 0$$

write an anonymous function that returns its two solutions. Use a nested declaration to compute the discriminant of the solutions only once. Apply the anonymous function to find the solution of $x^2 - 3 = 0$.

Anonymous functions are useful in functional programming, but it is of course also necessary to have functions with names.

In Scala, all functions are objects. Therefore, we can declare/assign them using val. For example, we can declare previous functions (i.e., give them a name!!) as follows[2].

```
val  f1  =  (a:Int)  =>  2*a
val  f2  =  (a:Int,  b:Int)  =>  a+b
val  f3  =  (a:Int,  f:Int=>Int)  =>  f(a)
```

---

[2] This is not the only way used in Scala to *define* functions. We can use def. Both ways are not exactly the same and def is not properly speaking a way to define functions. That is why we start defining functions with val. This is further explained in Sect. 6.3.

Now, we can apply these functions to objects in a more usual way. E.g., we can compute

```
f1(3)
f2(5,8)
f3(10,f1)
```

As a summary, we have that the definition of a function follows this structure:

```
val name = <anonymous-function-definition>
```

2.6.1 Alternative Ways to Define Types in Functions

When we use a definition of the form above, the information on the types of involved parameters is in the anonymous function.

We can also give the information about the type on the name of the function. For example, function f1 receives an Int and returns an Int. This is expressed in Scala as (Int => Int). The following three definitions are all valid in Scala for f1. Note that the third one contains redundant information, as the type of parameter a is given twice.

```
val f1 = (a:Int) => 2*a
val f1:(Int => Int) = a => 2*a
val f1:(Int => Int) = (a:Int) => 2*a
```

Similarly, we can define functions f2 and f3 above as follows:

```
val f2:((Int,Int)=>Int) = (a:Int, b:Int) => a+b
val f2:((Int,Int)=>Int) = (a, b) => a+b
val f3:((Int,Int=>Int)=>Int) = (a:Int, f:Int=>Int) => f(a)
val f3:((Int,Int=>Int)=>Int) = (a, f) => f(a)
```

Type definition in functions. Scala permits different ways to express the type of a function. It is usually **more convenient** to associate types to functions than to their parameters. That is, among the alternatives seen, the most convenient way to define a function is to follow this pattern:

```
val name: FunctionType = <anonymous-function-definition>
```

2.6.2 Type Inference in Scala

A type inference system permits to conclude the types of objects and functions from their definition. There are languages as Standard ML where the type inference system is very advanced.

Scala has a limited type inference system. For example, the following definition without types is valid (because Scala infers the type of f4 from the type of f1).

```
val f4 = a => f1(a)
```

Nevertheless, the following two definitions return an error because the type is not given.

```
val f5 = a => 3*a
val f6 = a => 2*f1(a)
```

Type inference in Standard ML. Standard ML (SML) has a more elaborated type inference system than Scala. It accepts the following two definitions for f5 and f6, and infers correct types for them. If we type in the SML interpreter
```
fun f5(a) = 3*a;
fun f6(a,f1) = 2*f1(a);
```
We obtain:
```
val f5 = fn: int -> int
val f6 = fn: 'a * ('a -> int) -> int
```
where 'a means that any type is valid.
Observe that Scala needs type declarations here.

2.6.3 Signature

The signature of a function corresponds to a description of the types involved in the inputs and output of the function. That is, the types of its arguments (inputs) and its result (output).

Signature of a function. In general, the type of a function is
```
Type1, Type2, ..., TypeN => OutputType
```
However, note that TypeI and OutputType can correspond to types of functions.

To illustrate that in the signature we may need to express that some parameters are functions, we can consider the following signature.

```
((Int,Int)=>(Int => Int),(Int=>Int),Int,Int,Int)=>Int
```

This is valid for a function type. For example, the following function f7 has this type.

```
val f7:((Int,Int)=>(Int=>Int),(Int=>Int),Int,Int,Int)=>Int=
(f:(Int,Int)=>(Int => Int),g:(Int=>Int),a:Int,b:Int,c:Int)=>
    f(g(a),g(b))(c)
```

Note that this function has five arguments, two of them are functions, and three are integers. We apply f7 below to two functions (one defined with name ff and the other anonymous) and three integers.

```
val ff:((Int,Int)=>(Int => Int)) = (a,b) => (x:Int) => a+b+x
f7 (ff, (x:Int) =>2*x, 1,2,3)
```

Note that in Scala we need to declare the types.

Inference in Standard ML. In Standard ML it suffices to define:
  fun f7Then(f,g,a,b,c)=f(g(a),g(b))(c);
Standard ML infers for f7 the following type:
  val f7 = fn : ('a * 'a -> 'b -> 'c) * ('d -> 'a) *
                'd * 'd * 'b -> 'c
The computation of the expression above in Standard ML is:
  fun ff(a,b)= (fn x => a+b+x);
  f7 (ff,fn x => 2*x, 1, 2; 3);

2.6.4 Referentially Transparent

Given an expression e, we say that e is *referentially transparent* when we can replace the expression e by its value in all occurrences of e in the program without affecting the result of the program.

A pure function is a function that given the same input values, the output value is always the same, and there are no side effects.

Side effect. An expression has side effects when in addition to its evaluation it modifies somehow the state of the machine (e.g., update global variables, print values in the screen or to a file).

Note that this is not always the case in imperative languages, as functions can have a state, and then the output of the function can change even if we do not change the input.

Random number generators are typical examples of non pure functions. For example, in Java, the functions nextInt() and nextInt(int n) of class java.util.Random are not pure. Note that different applications of these functions may result into different results. Precisely, this is the goal of the random genera-tor function, that different values are obtained. Functions and methods applied to objects with internal states are usually not pure (as the state is not explicitly stated in the function). An explicit random state as e.g. in the call `randomState.nextInt()` could return a new random state and the random number, being a pure function.

The expression `println` in Scala is also not pure. Although its result is always of type Unit[3], it has a side effect. That is, the expression prints a string onto the screen.

> **Referentially transparent.** An expression satisfies this property when it can be replaced by its evaluation without modifying the outcome of the program. Expressions with side effects are not referentially transparent.

2.6.5   Higher-Order Functions

We have a higher-order function when one of its parameter is another function. This is the case of function `f3` above. Recall that it requires a function with signature (`Int=>Int`) as a parameter.

For example, the arithmetic mean of two values a and b corresponds to

$$(a + b)/2$$

and the quasi-arithmetic mean is defined for a function f with inverse f^{-1} as

$$f^{-1}((f(a) + f(b))/2).$$

We can implement the quasi-arithmetic mean [18] as a higher-order function `qam` with parameters `a` and `b` and two functions f and f^{-1}. We call this later function `fm1` in the definition below.

```
val qam:((Double,Double,Double=>Double,Double=>Double)=>Double) =
  (a,b,f,fm1) => fm1((f(a)+f(b))/2)
```

Then, we can compute the quasi-arithmetic mean of 1 and 2 with $f(x) = x$ and $f^{-1}(x) = x$ as follows[4].

```
qam(1,2,(x:Double) => x,(x:Double) => x)
```

Similarly, the quasi-arithmetic mean of 1 and 2 with $f(x) = x^2$ and $f^{-1}(x) = \sqrt{x}$ is computed by[5]:

```
qam(1,2,(x:Double) => x*x,(x:Double) => math.sqrt(x))
```

---

[3]Check the value of `pln` after declaring
`val pln = println("println is pure?")`.
[4]The quasi-arithmetic mean with $f(x) = x$ is just the arithmetic mean.
[5]The quasi-arithmetic mean with $f(x) = x^2$ is the geometric mean.

We use higher-order functions when we need some generality in our definition. For example, if we want to order the elements of a database but we do not want to establish how to compare pairs of elements we can use a higher-order function where the comparison (e.g., lessThan) is one of the parameters of the ordering method. We will then be able to compare and order in different ways. For example, by surname, or by city.

2.6.6   Currification

Any function of n parameters can be seen as a function that has a single parameter, and given it, it returns a function with $n - 1$ parameters.

Currification is the technique for making this transformation.

As an example of Currification, observe that we can define the arithmetic mean as a function of two arguments as follows:

```
val am: ((Double, Double) => Double) = (a,b) => (a+b)/2
```

but also as a function of one argument that returns another function that given one argument it computes the mean of this argument with the previous one. That is,

```
val curryAm: (Double => (Double => Double)) =
   (a) => { (b) => (a+b)/2 }
```

The way to call these functions will be different. We will use:

```
am(2,5)
curryAm(2)(5)
```

The main and important difference between currified and non currified is that we can call the latter with only some of the first arguments. For example, the following call is valid:

```
curryAm(2)
```

This call returns a function that computes the mean of any number with 2. We can thus define

```
val meanWith2 = curryAm(2)
```

and then apply this function to any other number as e.g.

```
meanWith2(10)
```

Let us consider a function to calculate the compound interest of a sum. The expression of the total accumulated value when the initial amount was P (the principal sum) and the total is to be computed for t years at a i nominal interest rate compounded annually is the following:

$$P(1 + i)^t$$

We can write this function in Scala as follows.

```
val compoundInterest: ((Double, Double, Double) => Double) =
  (i,t,p) => p*Math.pow(1+i,t)
```

Then, if we want to compute the balance after 5 years of 1000 Euros at 2.5 % of annual interest, we can call this function as:

```
compoundInterest(0.025, 5, 1000)
```

We give now the function in currified form and give also an example of its application.

```
val compoundInterest:
  (Double => (Double => (Double => Double))) =
    (i) => { (t) => { (p) => { p*Math.pow(1+i,t) } } }
compoundInterest(0.025)(5)(1000)
```

When the function is currified we can define a new function that computes the compound for any value when the interest and the number of years are known. For example, let us consider that today we have a 3 % interest and 4 years. Then, we can define a function compound interest to any principal sum. We give an example below and its application to 1000 euros. Naturally, once we have this function, we can apply it to any amount of money.

```
val ourBankInterestTodayAt4Years = compoundInterest(0.03)(4)
ourBankInterestTodayAt4Years(1000)
```

Currified functions are helpful to us because we can apply them only partially, which gives us additional flexibility.

2.6.7 Recursive Functions

In functional programming repetition is usually implemented by means of recursion. Recall that a function is recursive when it calls to itself.

Iteration and loops are avoided in functional programming because they rely on variables that change their state. Let us compare the definition of the factorial using loops and using recursion.

Recall that the factorial of zero is defined as 1, and then in general the factorial of an integer number $n > 0$ is defined as n multiplied by the factorial of $n - 1$. The mathematical expression for the factorial is, therefore.

$$fact(n) = \begin{cases} 1 & \text{if } n = 0 \\ n \cdot fact(n - 1) & \text{if } n > 0 \end{cases}$$

Using this definition, it is straightforward to define the recursive form of the factorial.

In Scala, when we define a function recursively we need to declare its type. Because of that, in the definition of factorial we express that this function receives an Int and computes another Int. Recall that this is expressed as (Int => Int). Then, the body of the function distinguishes by means of an if the base case (i.e., when $n = 0$) that directly returns the value of the factorial (i.e., $fact(0) = 1$) and the recursive case that computes $n \cdot fact(n - 1)$. The corresponding code in Scala is, thus, as follows.

```
val fact:(Int=>Int) =
  (n:Int) => { if (n==0) {1} else {n*fact(n-1)}}
```

or, equivalently, without giving the type of n:

```
val fact:(Int=>Int) =
  (n) => { if (n==0) {1} else {n*fact(n-1)}}
```

It is well known that the factorial is equivalently defined by the following expression.

$$fact(n) = \prod_{i=1}^{n} i$$

That both expressions are equivalent is proven by induction but this is out of the scope of this text. See e.g. [17] and [14] for a reference on induction and proofs by induction.

This later expression is used in most imperative versions of the factorial function. In this case, we have a variable that takes values from 1 to n, and a variable that stores the partial results.

We can implement this version in Scala as follows.

```
val fact: (Int=>Int) = (n) => {
  var res = 1
  for (i <- 1 to n) {
    res = res*i
  }
  res
}
```

We can compare this definition with the iterative version studied in Chap. 1. Note that the function in Scala does not need a return statement as the last expression computed in the function is the one returned.

Recursive functions. They are functions that call themselves. Recall that recursive functions need to consider: (a) a base case, that is not recursive and that returns a value; (b) a recursive case, in which the function is applied recursively to an object that is simpler than the one received by the function. Simpler means that is more similar to the base case.

For example, the factorial has 0 as its base case, and the recursive case applies the factorial function to a simpler object (the original value less one, naturally $n - 1$ is more similar to zero than n).

Other typical examples of recursive functions are the function Fibonacci, and the function to solve the problem of towers of Hanoi. The straightforward implementation of the Fibonacci function is quite inefficient but it is useful to illustrate recursion.

Exercise 2.2. Define recursively the function Fibonacci and the towers of Hanoi. Use a pure functional implementation for the former. You can use some imperative (as e.g. sequences of `println`) for the later.

Recall that the Fibonacci series are defined as follows. $F_0 = 0$, $F_1 = 1$ and $F_i = F_{i-1} + F_{i-2}$ (for $i > 1$).

2.6.8   Functions and Non Functional Programming

When we define a function, we can include in its body any valid Scala expression. This naturally includes loops and blocks (with sequences of statements). We have seen an example above of the iterative version of the factorial function. When we have a sequence of expressions, the function returns the last one (we do not need an explicit return statement).

2.7   Lists

Scala implements lists. In a list, all objects should be of the same type. So, if we have a list of integers, formally it will be of type List[Int]. Lists have two constructors. `Nil`, which establishes an empty list, and `::`, which adds an element to a list.

The following are valid expressions.

```
val exampleEmptyList = Nil
val exampleListOne = 1::Nil
val exampleListThree = 1::2::3::Nil
```

The constructor `::` is right associative, so, `1::2::3::Nil` is equivalent to `1::(2::(3::Nil))`. We can also use the function `List` that can receive an arbitrary number of arguments to define a list. This is used as follows:

```
List(objects between commas)
```

Consider for example the following list.

```
val anotherExampleListThree = List(1,2,3)
```

These examples defined lists of integers. Similarly, we can make lists of strings as follows.

```
"First"::"Second"::"Third"::"Fourth"::Nil
```

In fact we can even mix the type of the objects when we construct a list. We can define, for example,

```
"First"::2::"Third"::4::Nil
```

Nevertheless, as all the elements of the list should have the same type, in this case, the type of the list wil be `List[Any]` because of the hierarchy of objects in Scala (see Sect. 4.1).

There are a few functions defined for lists. Some of them follow.

- `head` returns the first element of the list. E.g., `exampleListThree.head` returns 1.
- `tail` returns the tail of the list (the list without the first element). E.g., `example ListThree.tail` returns the list `2::3::Nil`
- `isEmpty` returns true if the list is Nil. E.g., `exampleListThree.isEmpty` returns `false`.
- `==` compares two lists. E.g.,

```
scala> anotherExampleListThree == exampleListThree
res24: Boolean = true

scala> anotherExampleListThree == exampleListOne
res25: Boolean = false
```

Note that in these examples we call the function `functionName` for a list `aList` using `aList.functionName`. This is because `aList` is an object of the type `List` and we are calling the method `functionName` for this object (i.e., sending a message to the object using object oriented terminology). In the last case, the notation

```
anotherExampleListThree.==(exampleListOne)
```

is also correct. In Sect. 4.2.1 we discuss with some details different alternative notations in Scala.

- Other functions include: `reverse`, `length`, `:::` (that concatenates two lists), `last`, and `sorted`.

2.7.1   Recursion on Lists

It is usual to process the elements of a list to find one (or all) that satisfies a property, to count them, etc. We have seen some of these functions above. We will show how to implement them here.

Most algorithms can be classified as either as a traversal or as a search on a data structure. We have search when we are looking for an object with a certain property. Once the object is found, the search is stopped. We have traversal, when we need to visit all the objects in the data structure. The same applies to lists.

- **Examples traversing lists.** We give below a few examples that need to traverse a list. They are the functions length, sum, and prod. The first one computes the length of the list. Then, sum and prod compute the sum and the product of the elements of the list. In all cases we need to check all the elements either to count them or to operate them. All of them are defined by means of recursion.

  As we need to traverse the whole list, the base case is always the empty list (Nil), and the general recursive case is applied to the list without the head. Note that when we remove the head, the list contains one element less and, thus, it is simpler and more similar to the empty list.

  The definitions follow.

```
val length: (List[Int]=>Int) = (l) => {
   if (l==Nil) { 0 } else { 1+length(l.tail)} }

val sum: (List[Int] => Int) = (l) => {
   if (l==Nil) { 0 } else { l.head+sum(l.tail) } }

val prod: (List[Int] => Int) = (l) => {
   if (l==Nil) { 1 } else { l.head*prod(l.tail) } }
```

  Check that these functions work properly testing e.g.

```
sum(exampleListThree)
prod(exampleListThree)
```

- **Examples searching in lists.** Let us consider two examples of searching. One that looks for a particular integer in a list of integers, and another that given a test function returns the first integer that satisfies the test function. For simplicity, this latter function will return -1 if the object is not found. We call these functions, respectively, thereIs and thereIsOneSatisfyingP.

  The signature of the first function is ((Int,List[Int]) => Boolean) as it receives an integer and the list and returns a Boolean. The signature of the second function is ((Int => Boolean, List[Int])=> Int). In this case the function requires the function p and the list, and returns the integer found (or -1). In order to test the function thereIsOneSatisfyingP, we define two additional functions. They are the predicates is2 and is3multiple that receive an integer and return true when it is 2, or a multiple of 3, respectively.

```
val thereIs: ((Int,List[Int]) => Boolean) = (e, l) => {
  if (l==Nil) { false } else {
    if (e==l.head) { true } else {
      thereIs(e, l.tail) }}}

val thereIsOneSatisfyingP: ((Int => Boolean, List[Int])=> Int) =
  (p, l) => {
    if (l==Nil) { -1 } else {
      if (p(l.head)) { l.head } else {
        thereIsOneSatisfyingP(p,l.tail) }}}
val is2: (Int => Boolean) = (x) => { x==2 }
val is3multiple: (Int => Boolean) = (x) => { x % 3 == 0 }
```

We illustrate now the application of these functions with the following calls.

```
thereIs(2,exampleListThree)
thereIs(5,exampleListThree)
thereIsOneSatisfyingP(is2, 1::2::3::4::Nil)
thereIsOneSatisfyingP(is3multiple, 2::5::8::9::Nil)
thereIsOneSatisfyingP(is3multiple, 2::5::Nil)
```

Predicate. We use the term predicate in this book as equivalent to a function that given an object returns a Boolean.

In a search problem, one base case typically corresponds to finding the element we are looking for. This is the element e in the first function (condition e==l.head) and an element that makes the test function p true in the second function (condition p(l.head)). In the case that the condition is true we return true in the first function and the element in the second.

The general case typically consists on a recursive application of the function to the tail of the list. When we are not sure to find the element, these functions have an extra base case to finish the traversal of the list. Usually, this is to check whether the list is empty. The first function returns false for this base case (there is no such element e) and the second function returns -1.

We give below another version of the function product. This function traverses the list multiplying the elements but at the same time searches for a zero, and if the zero is found it returns zero directly.

```
val prodV2: (List[Int] => Int) = (l) => {
  if (l==Nil) { 1 } else {
    if (l.head==0) { 0 }
    else { l.head*prodV2(l.tail) }} }
// Test of function prodV2
prodV2(1::2::0::4::Nil)
```

Recursive functions on lists. There are mainly two types of functions: traversal and search.

- In traversal, it is usual that the base case corresponds to the empty list, and the general case applies recursively the function to the tail of the list.
- In search, it is usual that the base case corresponds to the case of finding the element (and also to the empty list if it may happen that the element is not found), and the general case applies recusively the function to the tail of the list.

2.8 Pattern Matching

Functional programming languages often include pattern matching. Pattern matching permits us to differentiate easily among different cases of a given structure. In addition, it permits us to associate some of the elements of the structure to variables. This is obtained making two structures equal. In Scala, we use match for pattern matching. The general structure is as follows:

```
variable match {
  case FirstCaseExpression => FirstExpression
  case SecondCaseExpression => SecondExpression
  }
```

It is important to underline that in Scala, the variable should be instantiated. This means that it should be linked to a value.

When variable matches a case, the corresponding expression is evaluated. Pattern matching permits us to use variables in the case conditions. Then, if matching takes place, variables are bounded to subexpressions. These variables can then be used in the corresponding expression on the right hand side of the case.

To illustrate how this works, let us redefine the factorial function using match.

```
val fact:(Int=>Int) = (n) => { n match {
  case 0 => 1
  case m => m*fact(m-1)
}}
// Test
fact(5)
```

When we compute fact(5), first, n is associated to 5. Then, as we have n match the value of n i.e. 5 is compared with each of the case expressions. That is, first, we compare n=5 and the case 0. As the two values are different, this case fails. Then, we compare n=5 and the case m. As m is a variable, both expressions can be made equal when m is 5. Thus, we apply the right hand side of this case with m=5. That is, we compute 5*fact(4). In this way, we will obtain the result of the function.

2.8.1 Pattern Matching on Lists

Pattern matching is usually applied to structures. For example, to define functions for lists. In this case it is usual to distinguish between the empty list and the list with at least one element. In the examples given in the previous section, we used the conditional to distinguish between these two cases. We can use pattern matching for the same purpose. In this case, we can directly associate variables to the appropriate elements of the list.

For example, the following definition computes the length of a list using pattern matching. As in the previous section, we distinguish between two cases: the empty list and the case of at least one element. The first case checks whether the list l can be made equal to Nil. This is only possible if l is empty. The second case checks whether l can be made equal to a list hd::tl. Here, hd and tl are two variables and we will have that hd will be associated with the head of the list and tl to the tail. This association will only be possible if l has at least one element. The names of variables l, hd, and tl are all arbitrary.

```
val lengthMatching: (List[Int]=>Int) = (l) => l match {
  case Nil => 0
  case hd::tl => 1+lengthMatching(tl)
}
```

Note that in this definition hd is not used. Because of that we can just replace hd by the symbol _ which corresponds to an unnamed variable. The alternative definition is as follows.

```
val lengthMatching: (List[Int] => Int) = (l) => l match {
  case Nil => 0
  case _::tl => 1+lengthMatching(tl)
}
```

We redefine below the examples of sum and prod.

```
val sumMatching: (List[Int] => Int) = (l) => l match {
  case Nil => 0
  case hd::tl => hd+sumMatching(tl)
}
```

```
val prodMatching: (List[Int] => Int) = (l) => l match {
  case Nil => 1
  case 0::_ => 0
  case hd::tl => hd*prodMatching(tl)
}
```

Exercise 2.3. Use lists to implement a multiset. A multiset is similar to a set but in which elements can appear more than once. For example, {a, a, b, b, b} is a multiset. Implement the functions union, intersection, and count for multisets. Given a multiset and an element, the function count returns how many times this element is in the multiset.

Pattern matching in Prolog. In Scala when we consider `variable match { list of cases }` we need that the variable is instantiated (i.e., its value is known). This is not the case in all languages. Prolog is an example of a language in which variables to be matched do not need to be instantiated. For example, we can build a predicate that delivers a list of N elements. This predicate compares the variable `List` which is not instantiated with the empty list `[]` when N is zero, and with a list with at least one element `[_|Tail]` when N is larger than zero.

```
listOfN(List,0):-List=[].
listOfN(List,N):--N>0, List=[_|Tail], N1 is N-1, listOfN(Tail,N1).
```

We can test this code writing the following

```
listOfN(AListWith5Elems,5).
```

The execution of this code will return a list of 5 arbitrary elements (see below). That is, the five elements are in fact not instantiated and can be *associated* to any value later. In Prolog, variables starting with _ denote that they have no value associated.

```
- ?- listOfN(AListWith5Elems,5).
 AListWith5Elems = [_G2984, _G2987, _G2990, _G2993, _G2996] ;
 true.
```

In Scala's pattern matching the variables within `match` are considered as *new*. Because of that, if we are using `hd` in the `match` part and we have a `hd` as one of the parameters of the function, they are considered as different variables. In the solution of the following example we illustrate that this may cause problems if used incorrectly.

Exercise 2.4. Define a recursive version of the function `from(n,m)` with n and m integers. The function returns the list of integers from n to m. Assume $n \leq m$. Consider the use of pattern matching in the definition.

Exercise 2.5. Define the function `quicksort` that given a list of integers, returns the list of integers ordered (from lower to large). Give a recursive version using pattern matching.

2.9 Collections and Their Higher Order Functions

We have studied lists in Sect. 2.7. There are other types of collections in Scala. Some of them are mutable and some of them are immutable. We will review some of them here. We start, however, reviewing what mutable and immutable data structures are.

2.9.1 Mutable and Immutable Data Structures

We have an immutable data structure when we cannot modify its values. *Modification* is achieved by means of constructing a new data structure. This is the case of lists in Scala. In Scala, we cannot access the ith element of the list and change its value. We proceed defining a *new* list with a different value in the ith position.

For example, if we want to change the 2nd position of the list (1,2,3,4) by 20, we do as follows (check values of x and y after the following code):

```
val x = 1::2::3::4::Nil
val y = x.head::20::x.tail.tail
```

In this case x is the original list and y is the new list. We define y as the elements of x from the 3rd element and adding to the front the first one of x and the number 20.

Note that the same type of definition is valid if we use var instead of val (we can check the values of variables x and y after the following code):

```
var x = 1::2::3::4::Nil
var y = x
x = x.head::20::x.tail.tail
```

We have mutable data collections when we can access and modify the original structure. In Scala Array is a mutable data structure. That is, we can access a given position and modify its value. The following code permits to visualize that the array is mutable.

```
val x = Array(1,2,3,4)
val y = x
x(1)=20
```

If we check the values of Arrays x and y after the execution of this code, we see that both contain Array[Int] = Array(1, 20, 3, 4). Note that this was not the case with Lists.

In functional programming we prefer immutable objects, for the same reasons that we prefer constants to variables, and that we avoid loops. We consider that they are safer for programming and of a higher-level. We will discuss in Sect. 6.4 efficiency of immutable objects. Although at a first glance it seems that we need to copy the whole structure in order that a function returns an immutable object, this is not always so.

Note also that the way we modify a list and an array in the previous examples is different. The modification of an array was *an assignment* (and thus, imperative-like) while to *update* the list what we did was to build one with the first element, the number 20, and the remaining part. If x is a list, it is not allowed to do x(1)=20

Mutable and immutable objects. An object is mutable when we can modify (via assignment) one of its components. An object is immutable if no modifications are allowed.

2.9.2   Mutable and Immutable Collections

We list below some of the collections that exist in Scala. We will review them together with some of their methods. The language offers a large number of other collections and functions that we will not describe here. Aspects related to collections are defined and implemented in different places (including classes, traits[6] and modules). We will not go into these details. See Scala documentation for details.

- List. As we have seen above, we create them with Nil, ::, List. Recall from the discussion above that they are immutable.
- Array. We can have arrays of any type. Recall from the above description that they are mutable. The following code illustrates this type.

```
var myArray:Array[String] = new Array[String](10)
var my2ndArray = Array("Reus","Paris","London")
myArray(0)="This is the first position"
myArray(1)="This is the second position"
```

- Range. It represents a sequence of integers from a given number to another one (not included) with a given positive integer step. The construction n to m for integers n and m generates the sequence of integers between n an m both included. The construction n until m for integers n and m generate a similar sequence but with m not included. We illustrate below the answer of the system for to and until[7]

```
scala> val oneToTen = 1 to 10
oneToTen: scala.collection.immutable.Range.Inclusive =
     Range(1, 2, 3, 4, 5, 6, 7, 8, 9, 10)
scala> val oneToNine = 1 until 10
oneToNine: scala.collection.immutable.Range =
     Range(1, 2, 3, 4, 5, 6, 7, 8, 9)
```

---

[6]Traits are discussed in Sect. 4.8.

[7]Properly speaking, to and until are methods of the class integer that receive a single parameter. So, 4.to(16) is also a valid construction. See Sect. 4.2.1 for details. There are functions to and until with two parameters, the first one is the limit and the second the step. Thus, 4.to(16,2) returns the range with values (4, 6, 8, 10, 12, 14, 16).

- Set. We can define sets of any type of objects. See e.g. Set(1,2,3). Elements can only be once in a set. We can add elements to the set by means of + and remove elements by means of −. In addition we have union and intersect to compute, respectively the union and intersection of two sets.

```
val s1 = Set(1,2,3,4)
val s2 = Set(3,4,5,6)
s1.intersect(s2)
s2.union(s2)
```

- Map. It defines a mapping from values of type A to values of type B. That is, a map returns an object of type B given one of type A. The following operations are defined get (which corresponds to the application of the mapping), + (to add an additional element to the map) and − (to remove one of the elements). Consider the following examples.

```
val map1:Map[String,Int]= Map("one"->1,"two"->2,
          "three"->3,"four"->4,"five"->5)
map1.get("one")
map1 + ("six" -> 6)
map1 - ("one")
```

For these collections we can compute their head, tail and whether they are empty using isEmpty. For example, we can compute map1.head.

For each collection with name NameOfCollection we can create an object of this type from a set of elements by means of calling NameOfCollection with the elements as their parameters. We have already seen some examples above for lists, arrays, sets and maps. Details on why the code List(1,2,3), Set(1,2,3), or even Iterator(1,2,3) works correctly can be found in [22].

Exercise 2.6. Define a currified version of the function curryF that returns

$$a * (b + c)^2$$

The definition should be done so that the following two expressions work correctly.

```
curryF (2)(3)(1)
List(1.0,2.0,3.0).map(curryF(2)(3))
```

2.9.3 Some Imperative Construction on Collections

Given a collection, there are ways to process their elements in an imperative way. For example, foreach applies a function to each of the elements. The function is expected to have side effects, as foreach always returns an object of type Unit. For example, check that

```
val result = list1 foreach ((a)=>1)
```

is a Unit.

Test also the following, and observe that after the execution variable r1 is Unit
while r2 is 6 as the block returns total instead of returning the output of foreach.

```
val list1 = List(1,2,3)
val array1 = Array(1,2,3)
val range1 = 1 to 3
val set1 = Set(1,2,3)
val map1:Map[String,Int]= Map("one"->1,"two"->2,
  "three"->3,"four"->4,"five"->5)
val r1 = {var total = 0; list1 foreach {
  (i)=>{ total = total + i }}}
array1 foreach {(i)=>{ println(i+2) }}
val r2 = {var total = 0;
  range1 foreach {(i)=>{ total = total + i }}; total}
set1 foreach println
map1 foreach println
```

We have seen in Sect. 2.2 that we can do a for in Scala using the following code.

```
for (i <- 1 to 10) { statement }
```

Again, we need here that the statement has some side effects.

In fact, we can use for (i <- sequence) {statement} to iterate on
the elements of any collection. In the expression i is a variable that takes values in
all the elements of the sequence. We use this construction with different types of
collections in the following expressions.

```
for (i <- List("alpha","beta","gamma")) { println(i) }
for (i <- Array(("one",1),("two",2))) { println(i) }
for (i <- Set(1,4,2,4).union(Set(4,3))) { println(i) }
for (i <- Map("one"->1,"two"->2,"three"->3,
  "four"->4,"five"->5)) {
  println(i) }
for (i <- 1 to 5 by 2) {
  print(Map(1->"one",2->"two",3->"three",
    4->"four",5->"five")(i)) }
```

2.9.4 Higher-Order Functions for Collections

There exist a few important functions defined on collections that help us to apply
functions on their elements. We review some of them below. For simplicity, we will
focus on lists, and examples are mainly on lists and ranges, but they exist for the
other types of collections.

- map. This higher-order function permits to apply a function to all the elements of the list. Given the list l and the function f we apply the function to all the elements of the list using l.map(f). For example, we can compute the factorial of all the elements of a list of integers as follows.

```
val fact:(Int=>Int) =
  (n) => { if (n==0) { 1 } else { n * fact(n-1) }}
(0::1::2::3::4::Nil).map(fact)
```

If the function has type A => B, the given list needs elements of type A and map returns a list of elements of type B.

We can also use map to apply a map to a list. For example, using the map map1 seen in Sect. 2.9.3 we can compute:

```
val map1:Map[String,Int]= Map("one"->1,"two"->2,
  "three"->3,"four"->4,"five"->5)
List("one","one","two","five","two","one").map(map1)
```

- filter. It selects the elements of a list that satisfy a given function. Therefore, one of the parameters is a function that returns a Boolean. Let us denote the original list by L and this function by f, then filter returns a list with the elements that make f true. I.e., $\{l \in L | f(l) = true\}$.

```
val notMultiplesOf3:(Int=>Boolean) = (n) => {
  n % 3 != 0 }
(1::2::3::4::5::6::7::8::9::10::Nil).filter(notMultiplesOf3)
```

This returns List(1, 2, 4, 5, 7, 8, 10).

Note that we can use in filter any anonymous function. For example, to select the multiples of 5 in the range 1 .. 300 that are also multiple of 3 we can proceed as follows.

```
(1 to 300).filter((n) => { n % 3 == 0 & n % 5 == 0 })
```

- take. Given n, it selects the first n elements of the list.

```
scala> (1 to 10).take(5)
res8: scala.collection.immutable.Range = Range(1, 2, 3, 4, 5)
```

- zip. It combines the values of two lists building a list of pairs or tuples (each pair contains an element of each list). For example,

```
(1::2::3::4::5::Nil).zip(0::1::2::3::4::Nil)
```

This expression returns the following:

```
List[(Int, Int)] = List((1,0), (2,1), (3,2), (4,3), (5,4))
```

When the two lists are of different length, the resulting function has the length of the shortest one.

- zipped. It is similar to zip. In this case, given a pair of two lists, returns a list of pairs. For example, the following expression combines two lists.

```
(1::2::3::4::5::Nil,0::1::2::3::4::Nil).zipped
```

Compare this expression with the one above for zip.
We cannot visualize the whole structure, but we can see individual elements with head and tail and we can see the following. With

```
(1::2::3::4::5::Nil,0::1::2::3::4::Nil).zipped.head
```

we obtain

```
res81: (Int, Int) = (1,0)
```

and with

```
(1::2::3::4::5::Nil,0::1::2::3::4::Nil).zipped.tail.head
```

we obtain

```
res82: (Int, Int) = (2,1)
```

- partition. This function returns a pair of two lists on the basis of a predicate. The first list contains all elements that make true the predicate, and the second list contains the elements that make false the predicate. For example, the following code

```
val notMultiplesOf3:(Int=>Boolean) = (n) => { n % 3 != 0 }
(1::2::3::4::5::6::7::8::9::10::Nil).partition(notMultiplesOf3)
```

returns

```
(List(1, 2, 4, 5, 7, 8, 10),List(3, 6, 9))
```

- find. It returns the first element of the list that satisfies a given predicate. For example, the following code returns 1 (as it is the first element of the list which satisfies notMultiplesOf3).

```
val notMultiplesOf3:(Int=>Boolean) = (n) => { n % 3 != 0 }
(1::2::3::4::5::6::7::8::9::10::Nil).find(notMultiplesOf3)
```

The following example finds the first multiple of 7 and 5 among the integers below 100. It returns, of course, 35.

```
(1 to 100).find((n) => { n % 7==0 && n % 5==0})
```

- drop. This function returns the collection without the first n elements. For example,

```
scala> (1 to 10).drop(5)
res87: scala.collection.immutable.Range = Range(6, 7, 8, 9, 10)
```

- dropWhile. This function is similar to the previous one, but with a Boolean function. Elements are removed until the function becomes false.

```
scala> (1 to 10).dropWhile((a)=> a%5 != 0)
res89: scala.collection.immutable.Range =
   Range(5, 6, 7, 8, 9, 10)
```

- foldLeft. This function is used to combine the values of a list according to a given function. Let $[x_1, x_2, x_3, x_4 \ldots, x_n]$ be the list, then given a value e_0 and the function f the function `foldLeft` computes

$$f(\ldots f(f(f(f(e_0, x_1), x_2), x_3), x_4) \ldots, x_n).$$

In the following example we use foldLeft to define a function to add all the elements of a list.

```
val sum:(List[Int]=>Int) = (l) => l.foldLeft(0)((a,b) => a+b)
```

we call this function with `List(0,1,2,3,4).sum`. Note that we can just use foldLeft to compute the sum of elements of any list without defining sum explicitly. This is done as follows.

```
List(0,1,2,3,4).foldLeft(0)((a,b)=>a+b)
```

Let us consider the signature of the elements involved in `foldLeft`. Let us first assume that the elements of the list are of type A. Then, we have that f is a function whose second element is of type A. Then, note that the result of the function does not necessarily require to be also of type A. Let us use B for the type of the output of the function. Then, note that the first argument of f should also be of type B. Therefore `f: (B, A) => B`. Because of this, e_0 is also of type B and the output of foldLeft is also of type B.

Taking into account this fact we use `foldLeft` to transform a list of integers into a string with the numbers in characters:

```
List(1,2,3).foldLeft("")((a,b)=>a+
   Map(1->"one",2->"two",3->"three",4->"four",5->"five",
      6->"six",7->"seven",8->"eight",9->"nine",0->"zero")(b)+"")
```

- foldRight. Similar to `foldLeft` but elements are associated on the right. In the case of the sum, both `foldLeft` and `foldRight` are equally valid to define the sum.

```
val sum:(List[Int]=>Int) = (l) => l.foldRight(0)((a,b) => a+b)
```

- reduceLeft. It is similar to foldLeft but without the initial value e_0. So, it computes:

$$f(\ldots f(f(f(x_1, x_2), x_3), x_4 \ldots, x_n).$$

For example, we can compute the factorial of 10 as follows.

```
(1 to 10).reduceLeft((a,b)=>a*b)
```

- reduceRight. This is also similar to foldRight without e_0.

Scala permits to use wildcards in the anonymous function we pass to these higher-order functions. For example, we can replace (a)=>(x%5 != 0) by _%5 != 0, and (a,b)=>a+b by _+_. Note that in the first case we replace one variable, and in the second case two. The following expressions are valid in Scala and are equivalent to two expressions above.

```
val sum:(List[Int]=>Int) = (1) => 1.foldLeft(0)(_+_)
```

```
(1 to 10).dropWhile(_%5 != 0)
```

Observe that the use of wildcards here is different to their use in pattern matching, were the value associated to a wildcard was not considered.

Exercise 2.7. Given a list of natural numbers, add the positive ones (and ignore the negative ones).

Exercise 2.8. Implement the internal product of two vectors using some of these higher-order functions.

Exercise 2.9. Implement recursively first without pattern matching and later using it the higher-order functions discussed in this section.

2.10   List Comprehension

List comprehensions are expressions that roughly correspond to the description of sets in terms of the properties of their elements. For example, we write in mathematics:

$$\{y | x \in N, x > 0, x < 10, y = x^2\}.$$

The general expression for comprehensions in Scala is:

```
for (enums) yield { expressionOnEnums }
```

In enums we describe which elements are considered, and then we generate them with expressionOnEnums. For example, the following expression generates the elements in the previous set.

```
scala> for ( i<-1 to 9) yield { i*i }
res9: scala.collection.immutable.IndexedSeq[Int] =
                      Vector(1, 4, 9, 16, 25, 36, 49, 64, 81)
```

In a comprehension, we can have multiple generators. The following example adapted from [25] generates pairs.

```
for (i <- Iterator.range(0, 20);
     j <- Iterator.range(i + 1, 20) if i + j == 32)
   println("(" + i + "," + j + ")")
```

Chapter 3
Lazy and Eager Evaluation

When we call a function with a few parameters, we are used to the fact that each parameter is evaluated before the function is called. This is known as eager evaluation. We can also say that such type of function is strict.

We can define formally strict functions introducing the concept of bottom (denoted by $\perp$). We say that an expression evaluates to $\perp$ when its evaluation does not terminate, or throws an error. For example, an infinite recursion or a division by zero corresponds to $\perp$.

Formally, we say that a function is strict when any of its parameters evaluate to $\perp$ the function also evaluates to $\perp$. For example, + is strict in Scala. The following expressions all lead to $\perp$

```
(2/0) + 2
2 + (2/0)
(2/0) + (2/0)
```

A typical example of a non-strict function is the conditional. Let us consider the conditional expression as follows.

```
if condition { thenBranch } else { elseBranch }
```

Note that this function is not strict. When we have 5/0 in e.g. the `thenBranch`, we only have an error of the conditional when the condition is true. Try,

```
if (n==0) { 5/0 } else { 2+2 }
```

© Springer International Publishing AG 2016   37
V. Torra, *Scala: From a Functional Programming Perspective*, LNCS 9980
DOI: 10.1007/978-3-319-46481-7_3

for $n = 0$ and for $n = 1$. Of course, in one case the expression fails and in one does not.

This is so because the branches are only evaluated when needed. Note that if we implement the conditional as a (eager) function with three arguments, all three arguments will be evaluated before the execution of the function and then the function returns an error independently of the value of the condition. Let us try the following:

```
val conditional:((Boolean,Int,Int) => Int) =
                (condition, thenBranch, elseBranch) => {
  if (condition) { thenBranch } else { elseBranch }
}
val n=0; conditional(n==0, 5/0, 2/2)
val n=1; conditional(n==0, 5/0, 2/2)
```

Observe that now both calls to conditional lead to an error. In Scala we can define functions with arguments that are only evaluated when needed. So, if one argument is not needed, it will not be evaluated. This corresponds to the definition of non-strict functions. When an evaluation is not done because it is not needed, we say that we have a lazy evaluation.

Lazy evaluation. The evaluation of an expression is delayed until we need its value. Lazy evaluation is used to

- defer expensive computations, and to
- define infinite structures.

In functions, we can defer the evaluation of an argument using the symbol => when we establish its type (placing => before the type). For example, we can define the conditional above with lazy evaluation for the branches as follows.

```
val lazyConditional: ((Boolean, => Int, => Int) => Int) =
        (condition, thenBranch, elseBranch) => {
  if (condition) { thenBranch } else { elseBranch }
}
var n=0; lazyConditional(n==0, () => 5/0, => 2/2)
var n=1; lazyConditional(n==0, 5/0, 2/2)
```

Important. Laziness can only be expressed as associated to the name of the function. It gives an error if we place => in the parameters of the anonymous function[1]. See e.g.

```
val lazyConditional: ((Boolean, => Int, => Int) => Int) =
 (condition: Boolean, thenBranch: => Int, elseBranch: => Int) => {
  if (condition) { thenBranch } else { elseBranch }
}
<console>:2: error: identifier expected but '=>' found.
   (condition: Boolean, thenBranch: => Int, elseBranch: => Int) => {
                                     ^
```

---

[1]This is one of the reasons why we stated in Sect. 2.6.1 that it is more convenient to associate the types to the function and not to the arguments.

Exercise 3.1. Define a function switch with lazy evaluation that given an integer that can be either one, two or three, and three expressions selects the first expression when the integer is one, the second when the integer is two, and the third when the integer is three.

3.1 Parameter Passing

Parameters in Scala are usually passed by value. In this case, the function receives the values but the variable that contains this value cannot be modified. Observe the following error.

```
scala> val plusOne: (Int => Int) = (n) => {
     |     n = n + 1; println(n); n }
<console>:8: error: reassignment to val
           n = n + 1; println(n); n }
                ^
```

> **Pass by value.** We have pass by value when the function gets a copy of the parameter, or the value cannot be modified. In any case, any change the function could apply to the value is not reflected outside the function.

This is in contrast to parameters passed by reference. In pass by reference, the function can change the values of the variable. Instead of receiving the value, functions receive the address of the variable where the value is.

When parameters are passed by reference, we do not enforce referential transparency, because functions may have side effects. Functions not only return a value but can modify as a side effect the values of some variables passed as parameters.

> **Pass by reference.** We have pass by reference when the function can change the values of the variable. This is usually implemented giving the address of the variable to the function.

A parameter is passed by need when the corresponding expression is only evaluated when its value is needed. In addition, in case that the value of the expression is needed several times, it is only evaluated once. That is, the first time an expression is evaluated, its value is stored (catched/memorized), and if the expression is needed again, this stored value is retrieved.

Pass by need. We have pass by need when the function evaluates an expression only when needed. So, if it is not needed, the expression is not evaluated. In addition, once the expression is evaluated, its value is catched and reused if needed again. That is, parameters are at most evaluated once.

When the parameter is evaluated when needed, but every time is needed it is evaluated again, we say that we have pass by name. Scala uses pass by name to implement lazy evaluation in functions[2].

To see that this is the case, let us consider the definition of a function that takes an integer and multiplies this integer by itself and again by itself. Let this function be lazy in this parameter. Then, let us combine this function with another that takes a number and returns it after printing a message as a side effect. If we combine this two functions, we see that the message is printed three times in the screen. One for each appearance in the expression.

```
val passByName:((=>Int) => Int) = (a) => { a*a*a}
val printAndReturnInt: (Int => Int) = (num) => {
  println("We evaluate the expression");
  num
}
passByName(printAndReturnInt(5))

We evaluate the expression
We evaluate the expression
We evaluate the expression
res127: Int = 125
```

Pass by name. We have pass by name when expressions are only evaluated when needed, and each time the expression is needed, it is computed again.

3.2 Lazy Val

Lazy val is a lazy version of val, in which the expression is only evaluated when needed. To illustrate this we consider the definition of xEager and xLazy, one

---

[2]**Personal comment.** From a user perspective, I would have preferred pass by need in Scala. If you program in a functional way with no side effects it is unnecessary to reevaluate an expression everytime you find it. Of course, in case of side effects pass by need and pass by name can lead to different results.

using eager evaluation and the other using lazy evaluation, and then their use. That is, we execute the following code.

```
val xEager =
   { println ("Evaluation of the expression"); 1 }
lazy val xLazy =
   { println ("Evaluation of the expression"); 1 }
xEager + xEager
xLazy + xLazy
xLazy
```

The interpreter (REPL) gives use the following.

```
scala> val xEager =
   |    { println ("Evaluation of the expression"); 1 }
Evaluation of the expression
xEager: Int = 1

scala> lazy val xLazy =
   |    { println ("Evaluation of the expression"); 1 }
xLazy: Int = <lazy>

scala> xEager + xEager
res0: Int = 2

scala> xLazy + xLazy
Evaluation of the expression
res1: Int = 2

scala> xLazy
res2: Int = 1
```

We can see that the definition of xEager executes the code as Evaluation of the expression is printed just after val. In contrast, this does not occur with xLazy. This is only printed when we are using xLazy in the expression xLazy + xLazy. We can also observe that the code of the definition of xLazy is only executed once.

3.3 Streams and Other Infinite Data Structures

The language Scala includes an implementation of streams which is a class similar to lists but where the concatenation of an element to the stream is lazy. The two constructors of streams are expressed by #:: and Stream.empty. They have, respectively, the same role as :: and Nil. Streams have implemented both head and tail methods.

As streams use a lazy concatenation we have that only the expression of the head of the stream is computed. All other computations are pending until they are needed.

Consider the following expressions and their evaluation.

```
1 #:: 2 #:: 3 #:: Stream.empty
1 #:: (2/0) #:: 3 #:: Stream.empty
(1 #:: 2 #:: 3 #:: Stream.empty).head
(1 #:: 2 #:: 3 #:: Stream.empty).tail
```

Note that the second expression does not evaluate to error, because (2/0) is not computed. Consider and compare the following two expressions sLazy and lEager. The first one sLazy corresponds to the definition of a stream and as such we have that the concatenation is lazy and (2/0) is not evaluated. We have a correct assignment. The second one lEager corresponds to the definition of a list, and thus the concatenation is eager. This forces the evaluation of the three integers in the list. As the second one is 2/0 the evaluation of the expression leads to an error.

```
val sLazy = 1 #:: (2/0) #:: 3 #:: Stream.empty
val lEager = 1 :: (2/0) :: 3 :: Nil
```

Using streams, we can easily define all the integers from a given number. We define this recursively as follows.

```
val from: (Int => Stream[Int]) = (n) => { n #:: from (n+1) }
```

Of course, we could have defined similarly

```
val fromList: (Int => List[Int]) = (n) => { n :: fromList (n+1) }
```

But the difference is that while we can compute

```
val naturalNumbers = from(0)
from(0).tail.tail.tail.head
from(5).tail.tail.tail.tail
```

we cannot compute the following.

```
val naturalNumbersEager = fromList(0)
fromList(0).tail.tail.tail.head
fromList(5).tail.tail.tail.tail
```

Note that these expressions lead to error because the evaluation of the list, which is infinite, does not finish until the stack is full. Therefore, the functions tail and head cannot be applied.

Let us consider the definition of a stream containing all factorials. We can use our definition of natural numbers as input for this purpose. The definition follows.

```
val allFactorials: (Stream[Int] => Stream[Int]) = (nats) => {
  fact(nats.head) #:: allFactorials(nats.tail)
  }
```

Then, we can compute all factorials with

```scala
scala> allFactorials(from(0))
res31: Stream[Int] = Stream(1, ?)
```

However, as this is a stream with lazy evaluation only the first one (i.e., the factorial of zero was shown). To visualize the first 5 factorials we can proceed as follows.

```scala
scala> allFactorials(from(0)).take(5) foreach println
1
1
2
6
24
```

Nevertheless, the implementation above for the function `allFactorials` is quite inefficient (we are multiplying and multiplying again the same terms). That is, when we compute the factorial of the first natural in the stream we are not using any previous factorial. We can write a more optimal code reusing our results.

We use a local function called `allFactRec` that given the pair $(n, n!)$ builds all factorials from $n!$. Note that we can apply recursively this function obtaining all factorials from $(n + 1)!$. If `factN` is the variable equal $n!$, all factorials from $(n + 1)!$ can be computed as follows:

```scala
allFactsRec (n+1, (n+1)*factN)
```

Then, the list of all factorials from $n!$ are

```scala
factN #:: allFactsRec (n+1, (n+1)*factN)
```

Because of that, we define `allFactFrom0` as follows.

```scala
val allFactsFrom0 = {
  lazy val allFactsRec:((Int,Int)=>Stream[Int]) = (n, factN) => {
    factN #:: allFactsRec (n+1, (n+1)*factN)
  }
  allFactsRec(0,1)
}
```

The following exercise illustrates the application of two other constructions we have seen for sequences to streams. However, as the streams are infinite, they can cause the system crash (caused e.g. by the garbage collector).

Exercise 3.2. Let us consider printing on the screen the stream of *all* natural numbers, and the computation of the *last* natural number. Warning: note that this can cause the system crash.

3.4   Stream of Even Numbers

Let us consider another example. Let us define the stream of even numbers. Following our previous definition of natural numbers, we can define this as:

```
val from2: (Int => Stream[Int]) = (n) => { n #:: from2 (n+2) }
val even = from2(0)
```

We can test this definition as follows.

```
even.take(10) foreach println
```

Let us consider an alternative way to face this problem. Let us consider our previous definition for natural numbers. Let us denote this stream nats. Then, we can define the stream of even numbers adding nats to itself. I.e., with an abuse of notation that is

$$nats + nats$$

Note that the following is true:

```
    0   1   2   3   4   5   6
+   0   1   2   3   4   5   6
---------------------------------
    0   2   4   6   8  10  12
```

We can do this defining a function ssum that is a sum for streams, and use it to sum the two streams of numbers. This solution follows.

```
val ssum: ((Stream[Int],Stream[Int])=>Stream[Int]) =
   (s1, s2) => { (s1,s2) match {
      case (hd1#::tl1, hd2#::tl2) => (hd1+hd2)#::ssum(tl1,tl2)
}}
val from: (Int => Stream[Int]) = (n) => { n #:: from (n+1) }
val nats = from(0)
val evenV1 = ssum(nats,nats)
```

We can visualize some elements of the stream using.

```
evenV1.take(10) foreach println
```

We can give a more compact solution if we observe that given two streams

$$< x_1, x_2, x_3, \cdots >$$

$$< y_1, y_2, y_3, \cdots >$$

we can build a new stream

$$<< x_1, y_1 >, < x_2, y_2 >, < x_3, y_3 >, \cdots >$$

using the function `zip`. Recall that the function `zip` was introduced for lists and sequences in Sect. 2.9.4. If we construct these pairs from the list of natural numbers, and we add the two values in each pair, we will obtain the list $< 0, 2, 4, 6, \cdots >$.

To complete this, we also need a function to add the two values in each pair. We call this function `addPair`[3]. We call `evenV2` the second version of our stream of evens.

```
val addPair: (((Int,Int))=>Int) = (a) => a._1 + a._2
val evenV2 = nats.zip(nats).map(addPair)
```

We can test these functions with:

```
evenV2.take(10) foreach println
```

Note that we can simplify this definition using an anonymous function.

```
val evenV3 = nats.zip(nats).map((a) => a._1 + a._2)
```

3.5 Stream of Odd Numbers

Let us now consider the stream of odd numbers. Note now that the following holds:

```
    0   1   2   3   4   5   6        .
+   1   2   3   4   5   6   ...
-----------------------------------
    1   3   5   7   9   11  ...
```

So, we can use approaches similar to the ones of the stream of even numbers. In this case we combine (or add) `nats` with the tail of the same stream. This results into the following definition.

```
val odd = nats.zip(nats.tail).map((a) => a._1 + a._2)
```

---

[3]In the example we use the following definition for `addPair`:
```
val addPair: (((Int,Int))=>Int) = (a) => a._1 + a._2
```
Note that here, a is a pair, and a._1 is an expression that returns the first element of the pair, and a._2 is an expression that returns the second one. An alternative way is to define
```
val addPair: (((Int,Int))=>Int) = (a) =>
        a match  case (a1,a2) => a1+a2
```
In this case we decompose the object a by means of `match` in the two components and add them. Unfortunately Scala does not permit the following to directly destructure the pair in the two components.
```
val addPair: (((Int,Int))=>Int) = ((a,b)) => a+b
```
For comparison, Standard ML permits this type of structure in the pattern matching. Observe the following valid code in Standard ML:
```
val addPair = fn (a,b) => a+b;
addPair (2,3);
val addPairOfPair = fn ((a,b),(c,d)) => a+b+c+d;
addPairOfPair ((4,3),(3,1));
```

3.6   The Fibonacci Numbers

Let us now define the infinite stream with the Fibonacci numbers. To solve this problem we start assuming that we already have this list. Note that this assumption is usual when we define recursive functions!!

So, if the list is available let us call it F. Then, it is easy to see that we can add F with itself but shifting the elements one position. Let represent the elements of F (the Fibonacci numbers) by `<f0, f1, f2, f3, ...>`. Then, we have that the following holds:

```
    f0   f1   f2   f3   f4   f5   f6
+   f1   f2   f3   f4   f5   f6   ...
------------------------------------
    f2   f3   f4   f5   f6   f7   ...
```

So, it is clear that we have to add F and the tail of F. As the addition of F and tail of F is the Fibonacci serie from the second position (i.e., `f2`), we need to add the first two elements. Therefore, using an abuse of notation, our solution is:

$$defF = 0\# :: 1\# :: (F + tail(F)).$$

However, we need to translate this definition to Scala. Pairing the elements with `zip` and using the function `addPair` above, we can give the following definition.

```
val fib: (Stream[Int]) = {
  0 #:: 1 #:: (fib.zip(fib.tail)).map(addPair) }
```

Note that this problem is very similar to the list of odd numbers. In this case, the definition is recursive. As before we can replace `addPair` by the corresponding anonymous function.

Exercise 3.3. Define the infinite lists of even and odd numbers by means of filtering the list of naturals.

3.7   The Prime Numbers

We define now a stream with all prime numbers. Our solution is based in the Sieve of Eratosthenes. The function will receive a list of integers. We presume that the first element of the list is a prime number, and that the list contains the numbers that has passed the Sieve for values smaller than the first one. That is, that if we receive the list $< x_1, x_2, x_3, x_4, \cdots >$ we have that x_1 is prime, and that x_i for $i > 1$ are not multiples of any value x smaller than x_1 (i.e., $x < x_1$).

Then, given this list, the list of primes from x_1 consists of x_1, and then all the numbers that are not multiples neither of x_1, nor from numbers larger than x_1.

Now, if we take the tail of the list (i.e., $< x_2, x_3, x_4, \cdots >$) and we remove all multiples of x_1, we will have that the resulting list has a prime at the first position (because we do not have multiples of numbers x such that $x \le x_1$). As a consequence, we will have a list with the same structure that the one received in the function `primeFrom`. We use this approach to define the function `primeFrom` recursively. Informally, it is defined as follows:

$$primeFrom(< x_1, x_2, ... >) = x_1 :: primeFrom(sieveOf(x_1, tail(list)))$$

Now we define it formally in Scala. The function receives a stream of integers to build primes from them. We call this list `pf`. The first (i.e., `pf.head`) is the first prime. Then, we apply the function recursively once we have removed all multiples of the first. This filtering is done as follows: `pf.tail.filter (_ % pf.head != 0)`. Putting all together the function defined is as follows.

```
val primeFrom: (Stream[Int] => Stream[Int]) = (pf) => {
  pf.head #:: primeFrom (pf.tail.filter (_ % pf.head != 0))}
val primes = primeFrom(from(2))
```

3.8 Exercises with Streams

We close this chapter with some exercises on streams.

Exercise 3.4. We divide this exercise in two parts.

1. Given a row of Pascal's triangle (or Tartaglia's triangle) define a function to build a new row. Give a recursive version and a version using higher-order functions (i.e., using `map`, `reduce` like functions).
   Recall that given the row

$$[a_1, a_2, a_3, \ldots a_{n-1}, a_n]$$

the new row of the triangle will be

$$[1, (a_1 + a_2), (a_2 + a_3), (a_3 + a_4), \ldots (a_{n-1} + a_n), 1].$$

2. Define Pascal's triangle with all the rows.

Exercise 3.5. Different ways have been found to compute approximations of the number π. Several of them use an infinite series where the addition of its terms tend to π. That is, the more elements we add, the better approximation we have of the number π. In this excercise we consider two of these series, and compare their approximations.

Define the following series (an infinite sequence)

$$s_k = \frac{(-1)^k}{2k+1}.$$

This is known as the Leibniz, Madhava-Leibniz or Gregory Leibniz series.
  Define a function that computes

$$\pi_n = 4 \sum_{k=0}^{n} s_k$$

Define the following series (another Madhava-Leibniz series)

$$t_k = \frac{\left(-1\frac{1}{3}\right)^k}{2k+1}$$

and the function that computes

$$\pi_n' = \sqrt{12} \sum_{k=0}^{n} t_n$$

Define the following functions

- a function that returns the (infinite) series that compare the values of π_n with π (i.e., that computes the serie $r_n = |\pi_n - \pi|$, where $|a|$ represents the absolute value of a).
- a function that returns the maximum error for a given value of n. That is,

$$maxError = \max_{k=0}^{n} |\pi_n - \pi|$$

- a function that returns the difference of the two expressions for π. That is, the series $|\pi_n - \pi_n'|$.

Exercise 3.6. Consider the Hofstadter's Q-Sequence, which is defined as $Q(1) = Q(2) = 1$ and for $n > 2$ as follows:

$$Q(n) = Q(n - Q(n - 1)) + Q(n - Q(n - 2))$$

As an example, observe the following computation:

```
scala> qn.take(10) foreach println
scala> qn
res90: Stream[Int] = Stream(1, 1, 2, 3, 3, 4, 5, 5, 6, ?)
```

Define this infinite series.

Consider the sequence $Q(1) = Q(2) = 1$ and for all $n > 2$

$$D(n) = D(D(n-1)) + D(n-1-D(n-2))$$

Define a recursive function `dr : Int-> Int` that given a value n returns the value of the sequence (in this case without using the infinite series).

Define this infinite series using higher-order functions. We call this function `dn`.

Exercise 3.7. Define the function `interleave` that given two streams $s1$ and $s2$ returns another stream with the elements of $s1$ and $s2$ interleaved. E.g., if we call

```
interleave(Stream(1,2,3,4),Stream(10,20,30,40))
```

we should get the stream (1,10,2,20,3,30,4,40).

Exercise 3.8. Define the infinite sequence `seqSin` defined by

$$x_i = sin(i/2)$$

for $i = 1, 2, \ldots$ and `seqSinE` defined by

$$x_i = sin(i/2) + \epsilon$$

for $i = 1, 2, \ldots$ where ϵ is a random number in [0,0.1].

For this you can use `scala.util.Random()` and `nextDouble`.

Exercise 3.9. A time series can be represented as a sequence of data $x_1, x_2, x_3, \ldots$ for given times $t_1, t_2, t_3, \ldots$. A moving average is a method for smoothing time series.

For example, a moving average of order 3 is the time series defined by

$$x_i' = \frac{1}{3}(x_{i-1} + x_i + x_{i+1}).$$

A weighted moving average is similar to a moving average but in this case terms are weighted. For example, the weighted moving average of order 5 with weights $w = (w_1, w_2, w_3, w_4, w_5)$ is defined by:

$$x_i' = w_1 x_{i-2} + w_2 x_{i-1} + w_3 x_i + w_4 x_{i+1} + w_5 x_{i+2}.$$

We can then define the weighted moving average with respect to the weights $w = (1/14, 2/14, 4/7, 2/14, 1/14)$.

For a given (infinite) sequence, define (i) its moving average of order 3 and (ii) its weighted moving average of order 5. The weighted average should be a currified function with two arguments: the weighting vector and the original series.

Apply these functions to the sequence seqSinE and compare it with seqSin (both defined in Exercise 3.8).

Note. You will need to define the first elements of the sequences (when expressions for x_i' cannot be applied in an appropriate way).

Chapter 4
Object-Oriented Programming in Scala

Omnia quae in notitiam nostram cadunt aut
cadere possunt mundus complectitur.
Seneca, Naturales quaestiones II.III[1].

As we have already stated before, Scala is an object-oriented language. In my opinion, Scala is an object-oriented language that incorporates functional programming concepts, and provides them in the object-oriented paradigm.

In this section we review the major aspects of object-oriented programming in Scala. For a more detailed discussion of object-oriented programming see e.g. [8, 11] and for the particular case of object-oriented programming in Scala see e.g. [8].

In this section we mainly ignore the functional programming aspects we have discussed so far. In Chap. 6 we will discuss how these object-oriented aspects interact with the functional programming elements.

Standard definitions of class and instance (as in any other object-oriented language) apply to Scala. A class can be seen as a schema or template for instances. In other words, an instance is generated from a class following the structure defined in such class. In object-oriented programming, all classes and instances are commonly referred as objects, and in a pure object-oriented language all that appears in a program are objects[1].

A class is defined in terms of fields (instance variables or properties), and methods (or functions). The creation of an object of a given class is known as instantiation.

We also have relationships of subclass and superclass between classes. When we define a class κ, we need to relate it to some existing class. We state that this new class κ extends another one κ'. Then, this means that κ' is the superclass of κ, and, equivalently, κ is a subclass of κ'. This defines the relationships of "subclass-of" and "superclass-of". We also say that κ has a "is a" relationship with κ'. For example, we can define first the class person, and then the class student as a subclass of person. In this case, student is a person.

---

[1]Note that e.g. the language Java is not pure as basic types are not objects and they are not in the hierarchy of classes.

© Springer International Publishing AG 2016
V. Torra, *Scala: From a Functional Programming Perspective*, LNCS 9980
DOI: 10.1007/978-3-319-46481-7_4

These relationships are important because subclasses inherit the properties and methods of superclasses. That is, if κ' is the superclass of κ, then the properties and methods of κ' are available to class κ unless κ overwrites them. Similarly, if k is an instance of class κ, k has available all methods available for κ.

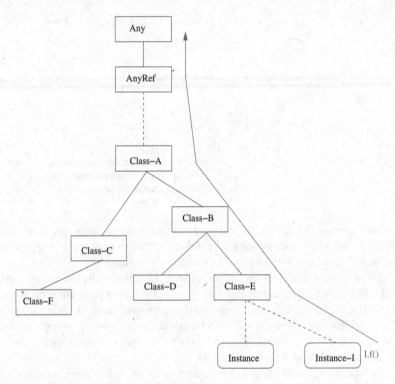

Fig. 4.1 Selection of a method via single inheritance

In a pure object-oriented programming, all actions are achieved by means of applying an appropriate method of one of the classes of the language. This is so, including e.g. the process of creating objects (instantiation).

Scala does only permit single inheritance for classes. That is, a class can only have another superclass. Because of that the set of definitions for classes define a hierarchy of classes, and this hierarchy has the shape of a tree.

Note that this is not always the case for object-oriented programming languages. In some languages multiple inheritance is permitted. In this case (observe C++), the relationships between classes define a directed graph instead of a tree.

Recall that in object-oriented programming it is usual to use the term message to denote the call of a function (or a method) from an instance of a class. We thus say, send a message f to an object o when we are applying method f of object o. This is usually written as $o.f$. If the method has arguments $a_1, \ldots, a_n$ we would use $o.f(a_1, \ldots, a_n)$. Note that this was the reason why we have been using ourList.hd to select the head of a list in our previous examples. Additional discussion on notation for methods is given in Sect. 4.2.1.

4.1 Class Hierarchy

Figure 4.1 represents the path Scala uses to find the suitable method when we call a function f of an instance I of class E. First, as methods are in classes, Scala will check whether f is present in class E. If it is there, this method will be used. If it is not there, using the inheritance relationships, a definition is looked for in another class. In general, as Scala uses single inheritance, if the function is not found in a class κ, Scala looks for the function in the superclass of class κ. The process stops in the class Any as this is the most general class. If there is no function in any of the classes looked, it means that there is no available definition of f for instance I.

In the hierarchy of Scala, the most general class, the one that encompasses all objects in Scala, is precisely this class Any. This can be observed if, for example, we consider the list with an integer and a string. Scala returns a list of Any.

```
scala> List(1,"string")
res11: List[Any] = List(1, string)
```

This is so because Any is the type of object that is superclass of both Int and String (and the less general of all superclasses of both). Then, there are two other general classes. They are AnyVal and AnyRef. AnyVal is the class that is the supertype of all value classes, which are the classes of the data types we have seen in Sect. 2.1 (i.e., Byte, Short, Int, Long, Float, Double, Char, Boolean, Unit) as well as other classes that can be defined by the programmer in an efficient way. The definition of new value classes is discussed in Sect. 4.3. AnyRef is the class that is the supertype of reference classes. Reference classes are all classes that are not value classes. The majority of classes are reference classes.

Two other special classes are Nothing and Null. Nothing is a subtype of all classes. It does not have any instance. Null is a subtype of all reference classes (subtype of all AnyRef subclasses).

Table 4.1 summarizes this information.

Table 4.1 Top and bottom classes of the hierarchy of Scala classes.

Any	The supertype of any type. Any object is of type Any
AnyRef	The supertype of reference classes
AnyVal	The supertype of value classes
Nothing	Subtype of every other type
Null	Subtype of reference types but not of value types

As we have seen in the example of a list with an integer and a string, it is useful to have the hierarchy of classes in mind. For example, in the next example, 1 : : a where a is a list of Nothing leads to a list of integers because the class Nothing is a subclass of Int. In contrast, as Null is not a subclass of class Int, the expression 1::b where b is a list of Null is a list of Any.

```
scala> val a:List[Nothing] = Nil
a: List[Nothing] = List()
scala> 1::a
res0: List[Int] = List(1)
scala> val b:List[Null] = Nil
b: List[Null] = List()
scala> 1::b
res1: List[Any] = List(1)
```

Note that if we add an object of type1 to a list of objects of type2, the list will be of type3 where type3 is the minimum generalization of both type1 and type2.

Observe, for example,

```
scala> val a = 1::2.2::Nil
a: List[AnyVal] = List(1, 2.2)

scala> val a = "zero"::1::2.2::Nil
a: List[Any] = List(zero, 1, 2.2)
```

4.2   Definition of a Class

As we have stated above, classes in Scala are defined in terms of fields and methods.

Fields correspond to instance variables. This means that each instance will have its own copy of the variables we define in the class containing its own value. Methods define how to operate the fields.

> **Class variables.** Recall that class variables are variables that are shared by all instances of a class. That is, all instances can read and modify its value. There are not class variables in Scala, a difference from other language as e.g., Java. You can use companion objects to have a similar functionality. Companion objects are described in Sect. 4.7.

The definition of a class establishes fields and methods, the superclass that is extended with the new class, and the parameters required by the constructor.

Constructors are the methods that are used to create instances, and each class in Scala has at least one (the primary constructor). The class establishes the parameters of this constructor including them between parenthesis in the class definition[2].

To define a class we use the following structure.

```
class NameOfClass [(parameters for constructor)]
                                    [extends AnotherClass] {
  bodyOfTheClass }
```

In this structure extends AnotherClass, which means that NameOfClass is a subclass of AnotherClass, is optional, that is why we have written this within square brackets. If nothing is included, the class extends AnyRef. The parameters are also optional.

The parameters of the constructor are expressed, in general, as follows.

```
var parameterName1: type1,
var parameterName2: type2, ...,
var parameterNameN: typeN
```

If no parameter is required, the list of parameters is empty. We have used here var, but both var and val can be used. As usual, they permit to define variables that are mutable or immutable. The following code illustrates this use. The code gives a first version of the definition of class computer and creates the object myComputer and modifies its fields. The class is a subclass of AnyRef as we do not include extends in its definition.

We can use private with a variable if we want to avoid its access from outside the class. In the example we only fix yearBuilt as private. It is well known that it is preferable to define variables as private to avoid missuse.

```
class ComputerV1 {
  private val yearBuilt = 2014
  var processor = ""
  var yearProcessor = -1
}
```

We can create a new instance of the class with new ComputerV1. In this case, the constructor has no parameter (and new ComputerV1() is also possible).

```
val myComputer = new ComputerV1
myComputer.processor =
  "Intel(R) Core(TM) i7-4510U CPU@2.00GHz  2.60 GHz"
myComputer.yearProcessor = 2014
```

We give now a second version of the definition of this class using parameters for the constructor. In this way, we can give values to the fields when the object is created. We can also use private in this definition.

---

[2]Auxiliary constructors are also allowed. They are methods implemented in the class with the name this. We include an example below.

```
class ComputerV2 (private val yearBuilt: Int,
                  var processor: String,
                  var yearProcessor: Int) { }

val myComp = new ComputerV2(2014,
  "Intel(R) Core(TM) i7-4510U CPU@2.00GHz  2.60 GHz",
  2014)
```

The following example defines the class Real. As no extends keyword is included, this class extends AnyRef. The class has a single variable re that the constructor will assign. We have implemented three methods. We have two methods to add and substract the object and another object received as a parameter. We have also implemented the method dist0 with no arguments. It computes the distance of the current object to zero. This is defined as the absolute value of the variable re. We also define the method toString, which is used to print an object of this type. As this method is already defined in the AnyRef class, we need to specify that we are overriding it. This is done with the keyword override.

```
class Real (val re: Double) {
  override def toString = "r"+re.toString
  def +(r2: Real): Real = new Real (re + r2.re)
  def -(r2: Real): Real = new Real (re - r2.re)
  def dist0: Real = new Real (re.abs)
}
```

We can observe that the definition of methods follows the pattern:

```
def name [(list of arguments)]: type = expression
```

In the methods, new Real (expression) creates a new real, that in our case are the output of the methods.

We have used re in the body of both + and −. This refers to object's variable re. We could also use this.re. Within the implementation of a class, this refers to the object that receives the call of the method.

With this definition we can create new numbers of type Real and operate them as follows.

```
val a = new Real(2.3)
val b = new Real(5.3)
a.+(b)
```

In a.+(b), we are applying the method + of the object a with the argument b.

Let us now consider the implementation of numbers of type Complex as an extension of real numbers. We include below its definition and two examples of its use.

The class includes a primary constructor and an auxiliary one. Secondary constructors are methods with the name this. In this case if we create a Complex with only one `Double` we will understand that this `Double` is the real part and that the other is zero.

```
class Complex (override val re: Double, val im: Double) extends
  Real (re) {
    def this (r: Double) = this(r, 0)
    override def toString = "c"+re.toString+"+"+im.toString
    def +(c2: Complex): Complex =
      new Complex (re + c2.re, im + c2.im)
    def -(c2: Complex): Complex =
      new Complex (re - c2.re, im - c2.im)
}
val b = new Complex(-2.3,4.4)
b.dist0
val c = new Complex(2)
```

We can observe that this definition inherits `dist0` from `Real`. We could redefine `dist0` if that was preferable.

Exercise 4.1. Redefine the class `Complex` so that `dist0` returns $\sqrt{re^2 + im^2}$.

Scala provides functions to find the class and superclass of an object. They are `getClass` and `getSuperclass`. We give an example below (the function `getAllSuperclasses` is based on [28]).

```
val a = new Real(2.3)
a.getClass
def getAllSuperclasses(cl: Class[_]): List[Class[_]] = {
  if (cl == null) Nil
    else { cl :: getAllSuperclasses(cl.getSuperclass) }
}
val b = new Complex(3)
getAllSuperclasses(b.getClass)
```

4.2.1 Notation

Methods can be called using the usual standard notation in object-oriented programming.

```
Object.MethodName(arg1, arg2, ..., argN)
```

However, the dot is optional, and the parenthesis is also optional in the case of a single or no argument. Because of that we can also use the following notation.

```
Object MethodName(arg1, arg2, ..., argN)
Object MethodName arg1
```

For example, the following pairs of expressions are equivalent in Scala. Note that we have been using the one on the right. The one on the left is the one with an object-oriented flavour. Note that the object to which the method is applied is clearly specified with the dot notation.

```
2.+(3)          2 + 3
2.==(3)         2==3
```

4.3   Value Classes

This type of classes have special properties.

1. They are extensions of the abstract class `AnyVal` (instead of being extensions of `AnyRef`). This is from Scala 2.10 (in previous versions they were a type of Trait, see Sect. 4.8 for traits).
2. Value classes are final, that is, they can not be further extended.
3. They consist only on a single value, and the value is directly held by a variable (instead of being accessed through a reference to the value). Because of that, the implementation of objects of these classes is more efficient.

Scala offers the following subclasses of `AnyVal`: `Unit`, `Boolean`, `Double`, `Float`, `Long`, `Int`, `Char`, `Short`, and `Byte`. The last seven ones are numerical. The first two ones are not.

Some examples of value classes follow[3]. First, an example for integers modulo 5.

```
class Mod5 (val intVal: Int) extends AnyVal {
  def +(m5: Mod5): Mod5 = new Mod5 ((intVal + m5.intVal) % 5)
  def -(m5: Mod5): Mod5 = new Mod5 ((intVal - m5.intVal) % 5)
  def *(m5: Mod5): Mod5 = new Mod5 ((intVal * m5.intVal) % 5)
  def ==(m5: Mod5): Boolean = (intVal % 5) == (m5.intVal % 5)
}
```

This definition permits us to define the values n1, n2, and n3 and compare them as follows.

```
val n1 = new Mod5(4)
val n2 = new Mod5(10)
val n3 = new Mod5(1)
(n1 + n3)==n2
```

Another example defining a class of real numbers follows. It is similar to the previous one in Sect. 4.2 but now we state that the class extends `AnyVal`. This makes its implementation more efficient.

---

[3]Recall that they are for Scala from version 2.10.

```
class Real (val re: Double) extends AnyVal {
  def +(r2: Real): Real = new Real (re + r2.re)
  def -(r2: Real): Real = new Real (re - r2.re)
  def negi: Real = new Real (-re)
}
```

However, as this class of real numbers is a subclass of AnyVal, it is final and we cannot define the class of complex numbers as an extension of the class Real. For example, if we prepare the following definition.

```
class Complex (val re: Double, val im: Double) extends Real {
  def +(c2: Complex): Complex =
    new Complex (re + c2.re, im + c2.im)
  def -(c2: Complex): Complex =
    new Complex (re - c2.re, im - c2.im)
  }
```

Scala returns the following error.

```
<console>:9: error: illegal inheritance from final class Real
  class Complex (val re: Double, val im: Double) extends Real {
```

4.4   Case Classes

Case classes is a type of classes with some specific characteristics. They provide by default comparison that can be used in pattern matching. We will discuss their use in Chap. 7 (Sect. 7.2).

4.5   Abstract Classes

Abstract classes are to encapsulate properties that are common to several subclasses. Methods in abstract classes do not need to be fully defined. This permits us to use abstract classes to force subclasses to provide certain functionalities.

In the following example we define an abstract class Number. We require that any Number has at least addition and substraction, and provides a type.

```
abstract class Number {
  type Self
  def + (r2: Self): Self
  def - (r2: Self): Self
}
```

Now we consider an implementation of the class Real that is a subclass of Number and later a class Complex that is also a subclass of Number. We provide examples defining objects and operating them. The classes provide the implementation of the object with appropriate variables, define the type `Self`, and implementing the methods required by `Number` (as well as other ones).

```scala
class Real (num: Double) extends Number {
  var re: Double = num
  type Self = Real
  override def toString = "r"+re.toString
  def + (r2: Real): Real = new Real (this.re + r2.re)
  def - (r2: Real): Real = new Real (this.re - r2.re)
  def - : Real = new Real (-this.re)
}
```

With this definition we can define and add two numbers.

```scala
val r1 = new Real(2.0)
val r2 = new Real(3.0)
r1 + r2
```

Another example of a numeric class follows. It defines `Complex`, also based on the abstract class `Number`.

```scala
class Complex (numRe: Double, numIm: Double) extends Number {
  var re: Double = numRe
  var im: Double = numIm
  type Self = Complex
  override def toString = if (im >= 0) {
    "c"+re.toString+"+"+im.toString+"i" }
  else { "c"+re.toString+im.toString+"i" }
  def + (r2: Complex): Complex = {
    new Complex (this.re + r2.re, this.im + r2.im) }
  def - (r2: Complex): Complex = {
    new Complex (this.re - r2.re, this.im - r2.im) }
  }
```

Similarly, we can define and add two numbers as follows.

```scala
val c1 = new Complex(2.0,3.0)
val c2 = new Complex(2.2,1.4)
c1 + c2
```

4.6 Singleton Objects

This is to define directly an object without defining previously a class. Alternatively, it can be seen as creating the class and its single instance. They are defined in the same way as a class but using the keyword `object` instead of `class`. The name of the object is the name of a variable containing this object.

Singleton objects permit us to organize functions (encapsulate them, make modules) when there are no variables in the object. It is equivalent to high level modularization. When variables exist in the module, a singleton can be seen as somehow equivalent to the use of static variables or class variables (or can be used for this purpose).

We can name a singleton object with the name of a class. Such objects are used to define companion objects. See Sect. 4.7.

4.7 Companion Objects

A companion object has the same name of a class. We can use them to implement functions to operate with objects of such class but that are not a direct application of a method to a given object. Note that when we define a class, methods are need to be applied to instances of the class. In the case of an object, we apply the methods to the object themselves.

We typically use companion objects to create objects of the class and to encapsulate functions that operate with objects of the class (but that are not directly applied to any particular object).

Consider the case of the class `Complex`, and a companion object of the same class. Then, if we consider a particular number `c` of type complex and functions `f` of the class and of the companion object, we will use `c.f` to apply the function `f` of the class `Complex` to the number `c` and `Complex.f` to apply the function of the companion object.

We must define a companion object together with the class, either in a file or using the `:paste` option in the interpreter. If we do not do so, we get a warning. Observe the following definition in the interpreter and the message obtained (we need to have defined already the class `Complex`).

```
object Complex {
  def sum (c1: Complex, c2: Complex): Complex =
    new Complex(c1.re+c2.re,c1.im+c2.im)
  }
```

The output of Scala for this definition is as follows.

```
defined object Complex
warning: previously defined object Complex is not a companion
    to class Complex.
Companions must be defined together; you may wish to use
    :paste mode for this.
```

Entering the following text to the interpreter (and adding a `^d` at the end of the text) we can define correctly the companion object. Note that in the code we define, one after the other, the class `Complex` and its companion object `Complex`. We can also put the definitions in a file (without :paste) and then load (or compile) the file. Note that these definition require the abstract class `Number`.

```
:paste
class Complex (numRe: Double, numIm: Double) extends Number {
  var re: Double = numRe
  var im: Double = numIm
  type Self = Complex
  override def toString = if (im >= 0) {
    "c"+re.toString+"+"+im.toString+"i" }
  else { "c"+re.toString+im.toString+"i" }
  def + (r2: Complex): Complex = {
    new Complex (this.re + r2.re, this.im + r2.im) }
  def - (r2: Complex): Complex = {
    new Complex (this.re - r2.re, this.im - r2.im) }
  }
object Complex {
  def sum (c1: Complex, c2: Complex): Complex =
    new Complex(c1.re+c2.re,c1.im+c2.im)
  def Eq. 2degree (a: Double, b: Double, c: Double):
                                      List[Complex] = {
    val d = b*b-4*a*c
    if (d<0) {
      return(
      (new Complex(-b/(2*a), - Math.sqrt(-d)/(2*a)))::
      (new Complex(-b/(2*a), + Math.sqrt(-d)/(2*a)))::
      Nil)
    }
    else {
      if (d==0) {
          return(new Complex((-b)/(2*a),0)::
                    new Complex((-b)/(2*a),0)::Nil)
      }
      else {
        return(new Complex((-b - Math.sqrt(d))/(2*a),0)::
                  new Complex((-b + Math.sqrt(d))/(2*a),0)::Nil)
      }
    }
  }
}
```

The companion object in this example defines two functions. One that adds two complex numbers and returns this addition and another that returns the two solutions of an equation of second degree. Recall that these two solutions can be either real or complex numbers. Our solution returns a list of two complex numbers. Note that we cannot define this method within the class Complex as none of its parameters is of type Complex.

The examples below show that we call this second method in the following way: Complex.eq2degree. Note that it is a method of the object Complex.

```
val c1 = new Complex(2.0,3.0)
val c2 = new Complex(2.2,1.4)
c1 + c2
Complex.eq2degree(3,2,1)
Complex.eq2degree(3,4,2)
```

Static methods and variables in Java. In Java static methods of a class cannot access to object variables, and they cannot call to dynamic methods. Static variables belong to the class and not to each object (there is only one copy of the variable and not one copy for each instance of the class).

Methods in a companion object can be seen as equivalent to Java's static methods. When companion objects include variables, they can be seen as equivalent to static variables. There is only a single copy of the variable, the one in the companion object.

In Scala Java's constraints naturally follow from the way companion objects are defined.

4.8 Traits

Traits are an alternative to classes. They can be used to define the signature of a set of methods and, in addition, to give a partial implementation of them.

In Scala classes have only one superclass. Traits can be seen as a way of permitting multiple inheritance, as we can define a class using several traits, and the properties of these traits will be inferred by the elements of the new class.

A difference between classes and traits is that no constructor parameters are permitted in traits.

We give an example below. We define the trait `Similarity`. It requires that any object implementing this trait provides a type and two functions. The function `isSimilar` is expected to compare two objects of the corresponding type returning a `Boolean`. The trait also implements the function `NotSimilar` in terms of the function `isSimilar`.

```
trait Similarity {
  type Self
  def isSimilar (x: Self): Boolean
  def isNotSimilar (x: Self): Boolean = !isSimilar(x)
}
```

4.8.1 Inheritance

Inheritance is permitted in traits, but only from other traits. For example, we can define the following trait that extends the trait `Similarity`.

```
trait SimilarityWithDegree extends Similarity {
  def isSimilarEnough (x: Self): Boolean
```

```scala
  def isNotSimilarEnough (x: Self): Boolean = !isSimilarEnough(x)
  def degreeOfSimilarity (x: Self): Double
  def selectSimilarEnough (L: List[Self]): List[Self] =
    L.filter(isSimilarEnough)
}
```

4.8.2   Multiple Inheritance

As we have stated above, we may have multiple inheritance of traits (in classes or
in other traits). This is achieved adding traits after the extends with the keyword
with. In the next example we define the class Point and the class Point3D
that extends Point and is forced to define the methods described in the trait
SimilarityWithDegree. Therefore, we have multiple inheritance.

The class Point3D uses three doubles to denote a point in the 3D space (x, y, z)
and a value epsilon that will be used to implement the function isSimilarEnough.

```scala
class Point (val x:Double, val y:Double) {
  override def toString = "("+x+","+y+")"
}

class Point3D (override val x: Double,
               override val y: Double,
               val z: Double,
               val epsilon: Double) extends
                 Point(x,y) with SimilarityWithDegree {
  type Self = Point3D
  def isSimilar (x: Point3D): Boolean = {
    return(x.x == this.x && x.y == this.y && x.z == this.z)
  }
  def degreeOfSimilarity (p2: Point3D): Double = {
    math.sqrt((this.x-p2.x)*(this.x-p2.x) +
              (this.y-p2.y)*(this.y-p2.y) +
              (this.z-p2.z)*(this.z-p2.z))
  }
  def isSimilarEnough (x: Point3D): Boolean = {
    return(degreeOfSimilarity(x)<this.epsilon)
  }
}
```

In this example, Point3D inherits the method toString from Point and then
needs to implement the types and methods required by the trait SimilarityWith
Degree. It also inherits the methods from the trait as e.g. selectSimilarEnough.
In the next example we test these classes.

First, we define some points.

```scala
val p1 = new Point(2, 4)
val p2 = new Point3D(2, 4, 3, 0.001)
val p3 = new Point3D(5, 9, 3, 0.001)
val p4 = new Point3D(2.00001, 4.0001, 3.000001, 0.001)
```

The following expressions show that we can display the point p3 using the method toString inherited from Point. Similarly, we can use the method selectSimilarEnough from the trait SimilarityWithDegree. We have also expressions to test the other methods.

```
p1.toString()
p3.toString()
p2.isSimilar(p3)
p2.isSimilarEnough (p3)
p2.degreeOfSimilarity (p3)
p2.isSimilarEnough (p4)

p2.isNotSimilarEnough (p3)
p2.selectSimilarEnough (List(p2,p3,p4))
```

4.8.3 Name Clashes in Traits

When two or more traits define the same method and we extend all of them we have a name clash. Observe that if we type the following code

```
trait First {
  def methodNameClash = 1
}
trait Second {
  def methodNameClash = 2
}
class NewClass extends First with Second
```

we obtain the following error.

```
<console>:9: error: class NewClass inherits conflicting members:
  method methodNameClash in trait First of type => Int  and
  method methodNameClash in trait Second of type => Int
(Note: this can be resolved by declaring an override in class NewClass.)
        class NewClass extends First with Second
              ^
```

We can solve the name clash explicitly overriding the method.

```
class NewClass extends First with Second {
  override def methodNameClash = super[Second].methodNameClash
  }
```

For completeness, we give the same example but using class for the first definition. The execution of this code will lead also to an error.

```
class First {
  def methodNameClash = 1
}
trait Second {
  def methodNameClash = 2
}
class NewClass extends First with Second {
  override def methodNameClash = super[Second].methodNameClash
  }
```

Recall that Scala does not permit multiple inheritance for classes, so it is not allowed that both are classes. If you test with two classes you will get an error.

4.9   Packages

Scala permits to define packages, which are only a way to encapsulate objects, classes and other packages. It is not possible to define objects with val or def within a package.

Given a package with some definitions, we can access these definitions using the notation packageName.definitionName. We can import all such definitions to avoid using the package name with import packageName._.

Packages are not first class objects in Scala.

The following example illustrates the use of packages. We have one package that contains a class, an object and another package. Then, we have an object that uses objects in this package. Let us paste this text[4] to the Scala interpreter (recall that we need to finish the text with ^d).

```
:paste -raw
package pName {
  class c1 {
    def print = { println("c1") }
  }
  object o1 {
    def print = { println("c2") }
  }
  package p2Name {
    object o2 {
      def print = { println("o2") }
    }
  }
}
object MyThirdFile {
  def test = {
```

---

[4]The keyword used below -raw is only available from Scala 2.11.

```
    pName.p2Name.o2.print
    0
  }
}
```

Then, we can execute the following code. This accesses the object o2 of package p2Name and uses its `print` method.

```
val a:Int = MyThirdFile.test
```

The output we obtain from the system is the following one.

```
o2
a: Int = 0
```

4.10 Some Additional Issues

As we have stated several times in this book, Scala is based on the Java Virtual Machine. Classes in Java can be accessed through Scala. Because of that, we have at our disposal a set of classes that can be useful when writting Scala programs.

For example, if we ask Scala about the class `Math` we obtain that the following methods are implemented. Note that we type `Math.` below but in order to get the output from the system we need also to press the `<tab>`.

```
scala> Math.
E                ceil              hypot             nextDown      subtractExact
IEEEremainder    copySign          incrementExact    nextUp        tan
PI               cos               isInstanceOf      pow           tanh
abs              cosh              log               random        toDegrees
acos             decrementExact    log10             rint          toIntExact
addExact         exp               log1p             round         toRadians
asInstanceOf     expm1             max               scalb         toString
asin             floor             min               signum        ulp
atan             floorDiv          multiplyExact     sin
atan2            floorMod          negateExact       sinh
cbrt             getExponent       nextAfter         sqrt
```

This output was obtained for a Scala version 2.11.6 and Java 1.8.0_91. Other versions may lead to different functions.

Chapter 5
Types and Classes Revisited: Polymorphism

We can define polymorphic methods using type variables. Polymorphic functions are those that can be applied to data of different types. Polymorphism is different from overloading that corresponds to have different functions with different types but with the same name. For example, addition + in `Real` and `Complex` are not polymorphic because we have two different functions with different implementations.

Type variables are added after the name of the method (in square brackets and in capital letters). Then, we can use these type variables when we define the types of the parameters.

The following example returns the third element of a list. We use A to denote the type of the elements in the list. Thus, the function receives a list of elements of type A. That is, `List[A]`. The function returns an element of type A. Our construction can be used for lists of any type. For example, lists of integers. In such case, we will have that A corresponds to `Int`.

```
def third[A] (l: List[A]): A = { l.tail.tail.head }
```

We can test this function with two different types of list as follows.

```
third(List(1,2,3,4))
third(List("one","two","three","four"))
```

Another example follows. It is a higher-order function `curry` that given a function with two parameters it currifies it. The most general case is when the two parameters of the function received by `curry` (say f) are of different and arbitrary types (say A and B) and the output is of a third arbitrary type (say C). We define the function below.

```
def curry[A,B,C] (f:(A,B)=>C): A=>(B=>C) = {
  (x) => (y) => f(x,y) }
```

We give examples of the application of this function. The first two definitions are equivalent. They differ in the way we inform Scala about the types involved in the

© Springer International Publishing AG 2016

V. Torra, *Scala: From a Functional Programming Perspective*, LNCS 9980

DOI: 10.1007/978-3-319-46481-7_5

function. Note that although the definition of `curry` uses three different types A, B, and C, we can have A=B=C=Int, as in the third example below.

```
val fc1 = curry[Int,Double,String]((a,b) => { "output string" })
val fc2 = curry((a:Int,b:Double) => { "output string" })
val fc3 = curry((a:Int,b:Int) => { a+b })
```

As the functions are now currified, we can call these functions with the two arguments or with only one. See e.g.

```
fc2(3)
fc2(3)(5.3)
fc3(2)
fc3(2)(4)
```

Exercise 5.1. Define a recursive version of the method `from(vFrom,vTo,gen)` which generates a list of elements where the first one is `vFrom` and the last one is `vTo`. These two elements are of an arbitrary type. Then, `gen` is a function that given an element of this arbitrary type generates a new one.

The function `from` starts with `vFrom` and generates elements with `gen` until `vTo` is reached.

Give examples of its application to generate lists of integers from 3 to 10, even numbers from 2 to 10, characters from a to k, and powers of 2 from 16 to 256.

Note. As `from` is polymorfic, because we can define it for an arbitrary type, we need to define it using `def`.

Exercise 5.2. Define the function `quicksort` with two arguments. The first one is a list of elements of an arbitrary type, and the second a function that given two elements of this type returns true when the first is smaller than the second. Then, quicksort returns the list of elements ordered (from lowest to largest according to the function).

5.1   Classes with Polymorphic Types

We can define classes that depend on types. This is done in a similar way as we do with methods. That is, adding a parameter to the definition of the class with its type.

In the following example we show how this can be used to solve problems with types in classes. We can proceed similarly with traits.

Consider the following problem. Let us add a method to the abstract class `Number` that when applied to a given `Number` adds this number to all the elements of a list and substracts another number. The signature of the method is:

```
def addThisSubstThat (a: Self, l: List[Self]): List[Self]
```

and we expect to apply it as follows

```
n.addThisSubstThat(a,[x1,...,xn])
```

obtaining the list

```
[n+x1-a,...,n+xn-a]
```

A first incorrect approximation to solve this problem is to define a class `Number` implementing this method and two additional methods + and −.

```
abstract class Number {
  type Self
  def + (r2: Self): Self
  def - (r2: Self): Self
  def addThisSubstThat (a: Self, l: List[Self]): List[Self] = {
    if (l==Nil) { Nil } else
      { ((this+l.head)-a)::addThisSubstThat(a,l.tail) }
  }
}
```

Nevertheless this definition does not work because there is a conflict with the types in the expression `((this+l.head)-a)`. This is so because a and `l.head` are of type `Self` while `this` is a `Number`. Observe the output of Scala for this definition.

```
<console>:13: error: value - is not a member of Number.this.Self
            { ((this+l.head)-a)::addThisSubstThat(a,l.tail) }
                             ^
```

This problem can be solved adding a type in the definition of the class. That is, the class depends on a type. We call this type `Self`, and we require with the code `<: Number [Self]` that this type is a subtype of `Number`. Now, we do not need to declare `type Self` as it is already known (because it is in the header). Then, we use `Self` to declare that the object (i.e., `this`) is of type `Self`. We need also to add `=>` in this definition.

```
abstract class Number[Self <: Number [Self]] {
  this: Self =>
  //  type Self: This is not needed now.
  def + (r2: Self): Self
  def - (r2: Self): Self
  def addThisSubstThat (a: Self, l: List[Self]): List[Self] = {
    if (l==Nil) { Nil } else
      { ((this+l.head)-a)::addThisSubstThat(a,l.tail) }
  }
}
```

Now we redefine `Real` extending this type of `Number`. We need to make explicit that `Real` extends `Number` when `Self` is `Real`. So, we use `Real ... extends Number[Real]` in the definition below. If we compare this definition with the previous one for `real` we also observe that we do not need to state now that `Self` is `Real`.

```scala
class Real (num: Double) extends Number[Real] {
  var re: Double = num
  // type Self = Real: This is not needed now.
  override def toString = "r"+re.toString
  def + (r2: Real): Real = new Real (this.re + r2.re)
  def - (r2: Real): Real = new Real (this.re - r2.re)
  def - : Real = new Real (-this.re)
}
```

We give an example of the application of these definitions.

```scala
(new Real(2)).addThisSubstThat(new Real(4),
                  List(new Real(1),new Real(2),new Real(3)))
```

We can proceed in the same way to implement `Complex` as an extension of `Number`.

```scala
class Complex (numRe: Double, numIm: Double) extends
                                      Number[Complex] {
  var re: Double = numRe
  var im: Double = numIm
  // type Self = Complex
  def this (r: Double) = this(r, 0)
  override def toString = if (im >= 0) {
    "c"+re.toString+"+"+im.toString+"i" }
  else { "c"+re.toString+im.toString+"i" }
  def + (r2: Complex): Complex =
    new Complex (this.re + r2.re, this.im + r2.im)
  def - (r2: Complex): Complex =
    new Complex (this.re - r2.re, this.im - r2.im)
  }
```

We also provide an example for this class.

```scala
(new Complex(2,3)).addThisSubstThat(new Complex(4,2),
      List(new Complex(1,1),new Complex(2,6),new Complex(3,5)))
```

5.2 Monoids, Functors, and Monads

In the way of greater genericity a few types of data have emerged as useful. We can see them as generic types with operations satisfying some properties. In Scala, we can define these generic types as (abstract) classes, objects or traits. Then, we can define higher-order functions on them, and thus apply them to actual objects.

The definition of these generic types can be seen as a scheleton of the type, because not all properties can always be explicitly stated in Scala. For example, we see below that a monoid is based on an associative function. However, if we define a trait for monoids we can require that there is a function for the type, but we cannot require that the function is associative. So, the satisfaction of this requirement is left to the programmer.

5.2.1 Monoids

This name comes from category theory [10], and in such context they correspond to a type of algebra.

In the context of object-oriented programming and Scala, they are types that include a binary associative function and an identity element for this function. Examples of monoids include:

- Integers, with the sum and zero.
- Integers, with the product and one.
- Strings, with the concatenation ("+") and the empty string.
- Lists, with the concatenation of lists ("++") and the empty list.
- Positive numbers, with min and zero.

Monoids are important because given a sequence of the elements of the type, we can combine them with the function in any order. This is because of the associativity of the function. Therefore, we can use the higher-order functions `foldLeft`, `foldRight`, `fold`, and `aggregate`[1] with any monoid. The result will be always the same.

5.2.2 Functors

We have seen in previous sections that one may define functions and classes that are parametric with respect to one or more types. This type of generalization can be pushed even forward.

Let us consider types as `List[Int]`, `Array[String]`, and `Something[A]` all containing different elements of a basic type (i.e., `Int`, `String`, and A) and implementing the function `map`. The function `map` given a function from the basic type to another (i.e., `f: A=>B`) transforms a `Something[A]` into `Something[B]`. We say that such type is a functor.

When applying functors from a set A to a set B, we expect that if on the set A there is an identity i_A and a function $f_A : (A, A) \rightarrow A$, and if on the set B there is an identity i_B and a function $f_B : (B, B) \rightarrow B$, then

---

[1] We will see `fold` and `aggregate` in Chap. 8.

- $f(i_A) = i_B$,
- $f(f_A(a, b)) = f_B(f(a), f(b))$ for all a in A and b in B.

We give an example of the definition of functor in terms of a trait, and two examples of objects satisfying the requirement of this trait.

```
trait Functor[GenericTypeOf[_]] {
 def map[A,B](gtype: GenericTypeOf[A])(f: A=>B): GenericTypeOf[B]
}
object ListFunctor extends Functor[List] {
  def map[A,B](list: List[A])(f: A=>B): List[B] = list.map(f)
}
object SetFunctor extends Functor[Set] {
  def map[A,B](s: Set[A])(f: A=>B): Set[B] = s.map(f)
}
```

Then, naturally, we can apply `SetFunctor.map` as follows (the map `fromStringToNum` was defined in Sect. 2.9.2).

```
val fromStringToNum:Map[String,Int]= Map(
  "one"->1,"two"->2,"three"->3,"four"->4,"five"->5)
SetFunctor.map(Set("one","two","five"))(fromStringToNum)
```

We can also extend `Functor` with new methods defined from the map. See e.g. the following

```
trait FunctorExtension[GenericTypeOf[_]] extends
                                   Functor[GenericTypeOf] {
  def composeMaps[A,B,C](gtype: GenericTypeOf[A])
        (fA: A=>C)(fC: C=>B): GenericTypeOf[B] = {
    map(map(gtype)(fA))(fC)
  }
}
```

This can then be used by any object or class that extends `FunctorExtension` once we define map. See e.g. the following example

```
object ListFunctorExtension extends FunctorExtension[List] {
  def map[A,B](list: List[A])(f: A=>B): List[B] = list.map(f)
}
```

Which can be applied as follows.

```
ListFunctorExtension.composeMaps(
    List("one","two","three","four","five")
  )(fromStringToNum)((i:Int)=>i*i)
```

5.2.3   Monads

A monad is another type that is useful in functional programming. The term also comes from category theory. Monads can be seen as an abstraction of the following example.

Let us consider a list of integers, its decomposition into prime numbers, and then the list of all primes. We will have something like:

```
List(2,10,15,45) => List(List(2),List(2,5),List(3,5),List(3,3,5))
                 => List(2,2,5,3,5,3,3,5)
```

We can see this computation in terms of a function f that given an integer returns the list of factors, and then a function flatten that given a list of lists of elements returns just a list of elements. If we generalize these types we have that we can use any type M[A] instead of the original list of integers, and the output can be any type M[B]. We use two types A and B as the function f could transform the type of the elements.

A monad is a generalization of this process considering the type M[A] (in our case a List[Int]), a function f from A to M[B] (in our case from Int to List[Int]), and then the function flatten that given a M[M[B]] returns a M[B].

A monad can be seen as a combination of a functor (we have M[A] with a map that permits to apply f to each element in M[A] and obtain M[M[B]]) and a monoid (that permits to flatten M[M[B]] into M[B] by means of the associative operator: e.g., concatenation in the case of lists).

In practice, monads are not defined in these terms but it is customary to define them in terms of the following two functions.

- unit. A function that given an element of type A returns an element of M[A].
- flatMap. A higher-order function that given a M[A] and a function from A to M[B] returns the data transformed into M[B]. That is,

```
flatMap: M[A] => (A => M[B]) => M[B]
```

The function flatMap is also known by bind. Scala has this function implemented. We could just apply

```
List(2,10,15,45).flatMap(decomposeNumberInPrimes)
```

if we have decomposeNumberInPrimes to decompose a number into its factors.

Monads are expected to satisfy a few properties. They are known as the Kleisli laws. For example that flatMap of m with a function (x)=>unit(x) returns the same m. However, we cannot force these properties into Scala.

Chapter 6
Scala: OOL and FP

In this Chapter we discuss a few issues related to the interaction between object-oriented aspects in Scala and functional programming ones. We also discuss some aspects related to efficiency in computation.

6.1 Tail-Recursive Functions

A recursive function is tail-recursive when the last action done by the function is a call to itself. Let us recall the recursive definition of the factorial.

```
val fact:(Int=>Int) = (n:Int) => {
    if (n==0) {1} else {n*fact(n-1)}}
```

This example is not tail-recursive because when $n \neq 0$, the function calls itself, but after doing so and obtaining the corresponding result it multiplies this result by n. We give below an alternative that is tail-recursive.

The solution computes the factorial by means of a tail-recursive auxiliary function. Let us focus on the auxiliary function. We call it `facttr`. The auxiliary function has two parameters. One that accumulates partial results. We call this parameter `acc`. We will proceed multiplying n by $n - 1$, by $n - 2$ and so on.

The other parameter is `n1`. It indicates what is still missing in the computation. We have that `acc` accumulates the products from $n1 + 1$ to n and what is missing corresponds to the factorial of $n1$. In other words,

$$acc = \prod_{i=n1+1}^{n} i$$

and, thus, for any $n1$ the following holds (this is an invariant of the function as it holds for any $n1$)

$$n! = acc * n1!. \tag{6.1}$$

© Springer International Publishing AG 2016
V. Torra, *Scala: From a Functional Programming Perspective*, LNCS 9980
DOI: 10.1007/978-3-319-46481-7_6

Taking this into account, the function `facttr(n1,acc)` will call recursively to itself as follows `facttr(n1-1,n1*fact)`. Note that

$$facttr(n1, acc) = acc * n1! = n1! * \prod_{i=n1+1}^{n} i$$

$$= facttr(n1 - 1, n1 * acc) = (n1 - 1)! * \prod_{i=n1}^{n} i = n!$$

> **Loop and recursion invariant** A loop invariant is a logical/mathematical expression that is true in each iteration. Similarly, a recursion invariant is a logical/mathematical expression that is true in each call. Invariants permits us to reason on the correctness of programs.

In addition to the recursive call, the tail recursive function needs a base case. The base case is when $n1 = 0$ (this case means that no computation is pending) and in this case we have that

$$acc = \prod_{i=n1+1}^{n} i = \prod_{i=1}^{n} i = n!.$$

Therefore, the base case returns `acc`.

Writing all together, we have the following definition.

```scala
val facttr:((Int,Int)=>Int) = (n1:Int, acc:Int) => {
   if (n1==0) { acc } else { facttr (n1-1, n1*acc) }
}
```

We can use this function to compute the factorial of any number n. We just need to call it as `facttr(n,1)`. Nevertheless, in order to avoid any misuse, we define a function `fact` that calls the tail recursive function, and make this tail recursive function local. The complete definition is therefore.

```scala
val fact:(Int=>Int) = (n:Int) => {
  lazy val facttr:((Int,Int)=>Int) = (n1:Int, acc:Int) => {
    if (n1==0) { acc } else { facttr (n1-1, n1*acc) }
  }
  facttr(n,1)
}
```

Note that in this definition we have added lazy to the local definition `facttr`. We need to use lazy otherwise the interpreter gives us an error as the function is local and recursive.

The importance of tail-recursive functions is that they can be optimized very easily replacing recursion by a loop. That is, the compiler does not need to allocate space for the stack (for the variables involved in the call). See e.g. [15] for a detailed discussion on tail-recursion.

6.1.1 Some Scala Technicalities

We can inform Scala that a function is tail-recursive using an annotation. We should use @annotation.tailrec before the function. Then, the compiler issues an error if Scala cannot transform your function using a loop.

However, if we add @annotation.tailrec in the definition above, Scala gives us an error because "lazy vals are not tailcall transformed". At the same time, as stated above, without a lazy eval, the local definition does work.

A way to solve this problem is that our local definition is a method instead of a function. The definition follows.

```
val fact:(Int=>Int) = (n:Int) => {
  @annotation.tailrec
  def facttr (n1: Int, acc:Int):Int = {
    if (n1==0) { acc } else { facttr (n1-1, n1*acc) }
  }
  facttr(n,1)
}
```

If you want to know execution times to compare implementations, you can use the function System.nanoTime and define e.g. function executionTime (that returns the execution time of a function f in seconds) and meanET (i.e., mean execution time of n executions of a function f) as follows.

```
def executionTime[A](f: => A) = {
  val s = System.nanoTime
  val ret = f
  val et = (System.nanoTime-s)/1e6
  (ret,et)
}
```

```
def meanET[A](n:Int, f: => A) = {
  (((1 to n).map((i)=>executionTime(f)._2)).
        foldLeft(0.0)((a:Double,b:Double)=>a+b))/n
}
```

With these functions we can compare different alternative definitions for the factorial. For this comparison we use BigInt so that we can compute larger factorials. The first one is with def. The second and third are with val and recursive (not tail-recursive). Difference is in the brackets. The last one uses tail recursion.

```
def factBId (n:BigInt): BigInt =
  if (n==0) 1 else n*factBId(n-1)
val factBIv: (BigInt => BigInt) =
  (n) =>  if (n==0) 1 else n*factBIv(n-1)
val factBIvc:(BigInt => BigInt) =
  (n) => { if (n==0) 1 else n*factBIvc(n-1) }
val factBItr:(BigInt=>BigInt) = (n:BigInt) => {
  @annotation.tailrec
  def facttr (n1: BigInt, acc:BigInt):BigInt = {
    if (n1==0) { acc } else { facttr (n1-1, n1*acc) }
  }
  facttr(n,1)
}
```

We can obtain their average execution time of 1000 executions for the factorial of 2000 using the following code.

```
meanET(1000,factBId(2000))
meanET(1000,factBIv(2000))
meanET(1000,factBIvc(2000))
meanET(1000,factBItr(2000))
```

6.1.2 Additional Examples of Tail-Recursive Functions

The following definition gives an implementation of the greatest common divisor (gcd) using Euclid's algorithm, which is recursive. As you can see, this definition is tail-recursive because the last actions done in the call is the recursive call. You can test the function calling e.g. gcd(10,20).

```
val gcd:((Int, Int)=>Int) = (a,b) => {
  if (a == b) { a }
  else { if (a > b) { gcd(a-b, b) }
    else { gcd(a, b-a) }
  }}
```

Let us consider again the Fibonacci series (see Exercise 2.2 and Sect. 3.6). Recall that $F_0 = 0$, $F_1 = 1$ and that $F_i = F_{i-1} + F_{i-2}$. However, instead of using a recursive definition using this last expression (which results into a rather inefficient and not tail-recursive implementation – Exercise 2.2), we will give a tail-recursive version.

To do so, we will use an auxiliary function that receives two consecutive elements of the series (f1 and f2 below), in each call if we have not yet reached the desired one, we build a new one and discard the smallest one.

You can see that this function is tail-recursive because the last action in the function is the recursive call. You can test this function using e.g. fib(6).

```
val fib:(Int=>Int) = (n) => {
  def fibtr (n:Int, f1:Int, f2:Int):Int = {
    if (n==0) { f1 }
    else { fibtr (n-1, f2, f1+f2) }}
  fibtr(n,0,1)
}
```

Exercise 6.1. Compare the execution times of the tail recursive and the straightforward recursive versions of Fibonacci.

6.2 Functions in Scala and Object-Oriented Programming

We have stated that in Scala functions are objects. In fact, functions are a particular type of objects which have implemented the method `apply`. The *application of a function* to an object corresponds to the execution of the method `apply` of this object.

See for example the following definition (ignoring for the moment the meaning of `Function2`). This expression creates an object that implements the method `apply` that given two integers returns another one.

```
val sum2 = new Function2[Int,Int,Int] {
  def apply(a:Int, b:Int) = a+b
  }
```

Then, we can call the method `apply` of this object as follows.

```
sum2.apply(2,2)
```

As we have stated, the application of a function corresponds to the application of the method `apply`, and that such objects can be understood as a function. Therefore, `sum2` can be used as follows.

```
sum2(2,2)
```

Scala documentation describes [24] that anonymous functions are a shorthand of the creation of a new function following the above example. In particular, it states that `(x: Int) => x + 1` is a shorthand of the following

```
  new Function1[Int, Int] {
    def apply(x: Int): Int = x + 1
  }
```

All objects are instances of a class. In Scala, functions are instances of anonymous classes. In particular, they are instances of anonymous classes which extend `FunctionN` traits, where `N` is a number. There are traits `Function1`,

Function2, ..., Function22. Function1 is for functions with one parameter, Function2 with two parameters, and so on till functions with 22 parameters.

See e.g. that the following anonymous function leads to an error because it has too many arguments.

```
(a01:Int, a02:Int, a03:Int, a04:Int, a05:Int,
 a06:Int, a07:Int, a08:Int, a09:Int, a10:Int,
 a11:Int, a12:Int, a13:Int, a14:Int, a15:Int,
 a16:Int, a17:Int, a18:Int, a19:Int, a20:Int,
 a21:Int, a22:Int, a23:Int) => a01+a022
```

Therefore, as a summary, if we create an object as an instance of FunctionN and it has implemented apply, it will be a function and behave like a function. If we try to create an instance of FunctionN but without a method apply, it will not work because the trait FunctionN requires that this method is implemented. E.g., the following code

```
val sum2 = new Function2[Int,Int,Int] {
  def other(a:Int, b:Int) = a+b
}
```

gives an error

```
<console>:9: error: object creation impossible,
           since method apply in trait Function2 of type
           (v1: Int, v2: Int)Int is not defined
      val sum2 = new Function2[Int,Int,Int] {
                 ^
```

Alternatively, we can consider just the definition of a class with the method apply. See e.g.

```
class something {
  var ourVar = 10
  def apply (i:Int) = 2*i
  def aMethod (i:Int) = i*ourVar
  def changeOurVar (i:Int) = { ourVar = i}
}
```

In this case we can have objects that can be called function-like but are just objects. See e.g. the following code. If we execute this code, the expression fakeFunction(2) returns 4.

```
val fakeFunction = new something
fakeFunction(2)
fakeFunction.aMethod(5)
```

6.3 Defining Functions Revisited: val and def

We have seen that both val and def are for declarations. We have seen that def permits us to define methods. First, it is important to underline that methods are not functions. Nevertheless, methods can be used as functions when needed. See, for example, their use in the higher-order function map below.

```
def add1 (n: Int) = n+1
(1 to 10).map(add1)
```

When we use def, the expression assigned with def is executed every time the definition is invoked. We can show that this is the case with the following definition.

```
def ffdef = { println("execution"); (x: Int) => x }
```

This definition has a side-effect. When we make the declaration, the Scala interpreter only returns the type of ffdef but the side-effect is not seen. The string execution is not printed. Then, every time we apply the method, the expression is evaluated and this causes that the string is printed on the screen. Observe the following.

```
scala> def ffdef = { println("execution"); (x: Int) => x }
ffdef: Int => Int

scala> ffdef(2)
execution
res8: Int = 2

scala> ffdef(2)
execution
res9: Int = 2
```

val permits us to assign an object to an identifier. As functions are objects (instance of a particular type of class), we can assign them by means of val. This is the approach we have followed in this text as it has a functional programming flavor. Recall that when we assign with val, values cannot be changed. We can use var instead if we want to change the value.

When an expression is associated by means of val to an identifier, the expression is evaluated. We need to underline that the expression is only evaluated once, and this evaluation is at the time we establish the binding. In fact, we already saw this issue when discussing lazy evaluation (see Sect. 3.2).

Let us define the following, analogous to ffdef above.

```
val ffval = { println("execution"); (x: Int) => x }
```

In this case, when we declare ffval, the expression

```
{ println("execution"); (x: Int) => x }
```

is evaluated, which implies that (as a side-effect) execution is printed on the screen, and then the object function (x: Int) => x is associated to ffval. When we apply this function, there are no (more) side-effects, as the function solely consists of (x: Int) => x. Observe the following execution, and compare it with the one above with def.

```
scala> val ffval = { println("execution"); (x: Int) => x  }
execution
ffval: Int => Int = <function1>

scala> ffval(2)
res10: Int = 2

scala> ffval(2)
res11: Int = 2
```

6.4 Data Types and Efficiency

We have seen in Sect. 2.9 that Scala implements both mutable and immutable classes. In particular, we have seen lists as an example of immutable objects and arrays as an example of mutable objects.

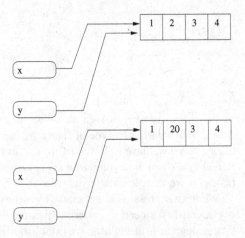

Fig. 6.1 Array(1,2,3,4) assigned to variables x and y (top) and the same variables after executing x(1)=20 (bottom).

First, let us recall that it is common to implement[1] lists by means of linked cells. Each cell contains an element and points to the next cell in the list. In the previous example, x will point to the first cell of the list (the one that contains the number 1). In contrast, arrays are usually implemented by means of contiguous positions of memory. We provide an illustration for the examples for both lists and arrays.

---

[1] Details on the implementation of lists are outside of the scope of this course. It is explained in books related to data structures (e.g. [1] and [4]). Look for topics on linked lists and linked structures.

Now, we will give two examples. One for lists and another for arrays. We start with the one for arrays. We will show the difference between mutable and immutable implementation, and discuss the issue of efficiency for immutable.

We consider the definition of an array, and its assignment to another variable. Then, we will update one position of the original array. This is expressed in the following code. Note that when we ask for the values of x and y after the execution of this code both contain the same array `Array(1,20,3,4)`.

```
val x = Array(1,2,3,4)
val y = x
x(1)=20
```

When we define that y is equal to x, we make y and x share the same position of memory (i.e., x and y contain the same pointer). See Fig. 6.1 (top). When we apply the statement `x(1)=20`, we are modifying the second position of this shared array. Because of that, if we ask for the values of x and y both will contain a value of 20 in the second position. See Fig. 6.1 (bottom).

Note, in addition, that the fact of assigning `x(1)=20` to x does not cause any problem even having defined x by `val`. This is so because the value of x is not really modified!! (recall that x is in fact, a pointer). It is only the content of the position what changes!

Let us now consider the case of lists. We proceed in a similar way, defining first a list, then assigning it to another variable, and finally redefining the original one. This is expressed in the following code.

```
var x = 1::2::3::4::Nil
var y = x
x = x.head::20::x.tail.tail
```

If we ask for the values of x and y after the execution of this code, we have that x corresponds to `List(1, 20, 3, 4)` and y corresponds to `List(1, 2, 3, 4)`. Figure 6.2 (top) illustrates the result of the two first lines of code. We have that both variables share the list.

Figure 6.2 (bottom) illustrates the result after the third line. We have that x and y refer to different lists.

Nevertheless, although x and y are different, it is not completely inefficient to proceed in this way. The usual implementation is that a list (when defined from another one) share elements. Note that we are building the new list x from the original x. More specifically, we add `x.head::20` to `x.tail.tail`. So, we can create the new list in a way that shares the elements in `x.tail.tail` and only the first two elements are new. In this way we do not need to copy the tail of the list when creating the new one.

In this example, we have that, after the execution of the code, variable y corresponds to the old list and variable x corresponds to the new list. At this point all cells are accessible from either one or the other variable. Nevertheless, it may happen that processing in this way some cells are no longer accessible. We can force such

Fig. 6.2 List(1,2,3,4)
assigned to variables x and y
(top) and the same variables
after executing
x.head::20::x.tail.tail
(bottom).

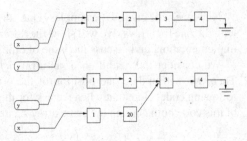

situation if we set y = x again. Now cells containing 1 and 2 cannot be reached because there is no pointer to the cell containing 1.

Note that once we have non accessible cells, there is no way to access them again. Scala does not offer a way to explicitly release these cells and let memory use them again. This is done by the language itself by means of garbage collection. Garbage collection[2] is the mechanism that is run by the language to find cells that are no longer accessible and made them available for reusing them later. In Scala, the garbage collection is done by the JVM.

> **Garbage collection.** Is the process of locating positions in memory that are no longer used so that we can use them again.

We will discuss the issue of data types and efficiency again in Sect. 7.3 with algebraic data types.

---

[2]Algorithms for garbage collection are explained in references and books on data structures. See e.g. the classical book of Aho et al. [1]. The first algorithm for garbage collection was implemented by McCarthy for Lisp and is described in [12].

Chapter 7
Algebraic Data Types

Algebraic data types are a concise representation of types permitted in some functional languages as Standard ML and Haskell. They can also be defined in Scala, and although their definition is more cumbersome, they are useful.

Formally, an algebraic data type defines a new type as a composition of other types or a set of possible constants.

In the definition of the type, we can enumerate the set of alternatives, some of them can be recursive. For example, we can define a type for the four suits in playing cards (spades, hearts, diamonds, clubs), the days of the week, the values in Boolean or in Kleene's trivalued logic.

We can also consider the product of these types. For example, to form a deck we have e.g. 13 cards per suit (Ace, King, Queen, Jack, 1, 2, 3, 4, 5, 6, 7, 8, 9, 10), and two jokers.

An advantage of algebraic definitions is that they permit to define functions by means of pattern matching.

7.1 Definition of Algebraic Data Types in Standard ML

The definition of algebraic data types in Standard ML is simpler and more concise that the same definitions in Scala. We give a few examples below using this other language. We will see how this works in Scala in the next section. The first example is the definition of the datatype suit. It just consists of four options.

```
(* code in SML *)
datatype suit = spade | heart | diamond | club
```

The next example is the definition of the type shape. It is based on the definition in [19] (p. 233). This definition corresponds to the definition of a composite type in terms of a disjoint union. There are three types of shapes: a point, a circle, and a box.

© Springer International Publishing AG 2016
V. Torra, *Scala: From a Functional Programming Perspective*, LNCS 9980
DOI: 10.1007/978-3-319-46481-7_7

```
(* code in SML *)
datatype shape = point | circle of real | box of real * real;
```

Then, we can define the area of a shape using pattern matching with these three same cases.

```
(* code in SML *)
fun area (point) = 0.0
  |   area (circle(r)) = 3.1415 * r * r
  |   area (box(w,h)) = w*h;
```

Then, we create objects and compute their area as follows.

```
(* code in SML *)
area(point);
area(circle(2.0));
area(box(2.3,6.9));
```

Exercise 7.1 Expand this type with a position where the shape is located, and redefine the function area.

Another type of definition is when we define types recursively. A classical example is the definition of the type list. If we consider a list ignoring implementation details, we observe that we can distinguish two major cases:

- the empty list,
- a list with at least one element, so the list is an element added to another (shorter) list.

Using this distinction, we can define lists recursively. We give their definition in Standard ML. The definition in Scala is in Sect. 7.2. As stated above, the list can either be empty (`emptyList` denotes an empty list) or a list with at least one element. In the latter case, a list of this form is composed adding an element of a certain type `'a` to a list of elements of the same type (i.e., an `'a list` using Standard ML notation). We add this element using the keyword `add`. Accordingly, the type is expressed as follows.

```
(* code in SML *)
datatype'a list = emptyList | add of'a *'a list;
```

The list with elements 2 and 6 is defined as follows:

```
add(2,add(6,emptyList));
```

Binary trees are another example of recursive data types. We can also represent trees by means of two cases, the case of an empty tree, and the case of a node with two subtrees (which can be empty or containing elements). In this latter case, the node contains an element of the given type. In Standard ML we can use the following definition.

Fig. 7.1 Example of a binary tree.

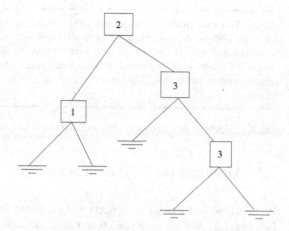

```
(* code in SML *)
datatype'a tree = emptyTree | node of'a *'a tree *'a tree;
```

We can represent the tree in Fig. 7.1 as follows.

```
(* code in SML *)
val tree1 = node(2,node(1,emptyTree,emptyTree),
                 node(3,emptyTree,node(3,emptyTree,emptyTree)));
```

We can see that these definitions for lists and trees do not focus on the implementation of the type. In addition, they consider the instantiations of the type as immutable. This, of course, does not hinder that we can operate with algebraic data types e.g. adding or removing elements of a list. Nevertheless, a function that removes an element of a list returns a different list.

For example, let us consider the following definition of removing an element from a list.

```
(* code in SML *)
fun remove e emptyList = emptyList
  | remove e (add(a,L)) = if (a=e) then
                             (remove e L) else add(a,remove e L);
```

If we consider the list x with elements 2 and 6, after removing 6, the list x will be not modified, and still contains 6. That is, if we execute this code:

```
(* code in SML *)
val x = add(2,add(6,emptyList));
val y = remove 6 x;
x;
```

Standard ML will return the list add(2,add(6,emptyList)).

Scala Documentation: Glossary [21]. Algebraic data types
A type defined by providing several alternatives, each of which comes with its own constructor. It usually comes with a way to decompose the type through pattern matching. The concept is found in specification languages and functional programming languages. Algebraic data types can be emulated in Scala with case classes.

Fig. 7.2 Algebraic data types according to Scala Documentation.

7.2 Algebraic Data Types in Scala

In Scala, we use traits, case objects and classes to implement algebraic data types (see Fig. 7.2). We use case objects to represent constant terms. In the case that we need to supply an object of another type, we would use case classes.

When we define an algebraic data type by enumeration, we need to use the following structure in Scala

```
trait NameOfADT
case object Name1 extends NameOfADT
case object Name2 extends NameOfADT
....
case object NameN extends NameOfADT
```

For example, we can define suits for cards as follows (note that the first line is a comment that just gives the definition in Standard ML and, thus, it can be omitted).

```
// (SML) datatype suit = spade | heart | diamond | club
trait Suit
case object Spade extends Suit
case object Heart extends Suit
case object Diamond extends Suit
case object Club extends Suit
```

When we need that the type is defined in terms of a parametric element, we need to use case class that extends the trait.

```
case class Name1 (arguments) extends NameOfADT
case class Name2 (arguments) extends NameOfADT
```

So the implementation of the type shape discussed above is as follows

```
// (SML) datatype shape = point | circle of real
//                                 | box of real * real;
trait Shape
case object Point extends Shape
case class  Circle (rad: Double) extends Shape
case class  Box (w: Double, r: Double) extends Shape
```

These definitions permit us to implement functions using pattern matching. We implement now in Scala the function `area` discussed above that for each type of `shape` returns its area.

```
def area (s: Shape): Double = s match {
  case Point => 0.0
  case Circle(r) => 3.1415 * r * r
  case Box(w,h) => w*h
}
```

We have seen that lists were defined as a recursive type with elements of an arbitrary type. This is expressed in Scala as follows.

```
// (SML) datatype 'a list = emptyList | add of 'a * 'a list;
trait ListOfA[+A]
case object EmptyList extends ListOfA[Nothing]
case class Add[A](head: A, tail: ListOfA[A]) extends ListOfA[A]
```

In this definition we need to establish that this is a list of elements of type A. We have the constant `EmptyList` (which is of type `ListOfA`) and the constructor `Add` that adds an element of type A (the head of the list) to another list (the tail) of elements of type A (i.e., this other list is of type `ListOfA[A]`).

We can define a list as follows:

```
val x = Add(2, Add(6, EmptyList))
```

The definition of algebraic data types by means of case objects and classes permits us to define functions by means of pattern matching, also for recursive types. In this case, we will need to consider the base case and the recursive case that follows naturally from the type. As an example we give the implementation in Scala of the function `remove` that makes a new list without all appearances of a given element. We have seen before its implementation in Standard ML.

```
def remove[A] (e:A, l: ListOfA[A]):ListOfA[A] = l match {
  case EmptyList => EmptyList
  case Add(a,tl) => if (a==e) remove(e,tl)
                    else Add(a,remove(e,tl))
}
```

The application of this function can be done as follows.

```
val x = Add(2, Add(6, EmptyList))
val y = remove(2,Add(2,x))
```

As in the case of Standard ML, the application of the function `remove` does not modify the original list x. Observe the following:

```
scala> x
res12: Add[Int] = Add(2,Add(6,EmptyList))

scala> y
res13: ListOfA[Int] = Add(6,EmptyList)
```

We give now another example of a stack. It is similar to the list. It uses an empty stack and a constructor that adds an element to the stack:

```
trait Stack[+A]
case object EmptyStack extends Stack[Nothing]
case class Push[A](top: A, rest: Stack[A]) extends Stack[A]
```

We can create a stack as follows.

```
Push(2, Push("a",EmptyStack))
```

We give now the function pop that returns the element in the top (if any). Note that the function is partial because it is only defined for non empty stacks.

```
def pop[A] (s: Stack[A]): A = s match {
  case Push(a,s1) => a
}
```

Observe the application of the function pop.

```
pop(Push(2,Push(3,EmptyStack)))
```

We finish this section giving the algebraic data type of a binary tree, and an example of these trees.

```
trait TreeOfA[+A]
case object EmptyBinaryTree extends TreeOfA[Nothing]
case class Node[A](value: A, left: TreeOfA[A],
                   right: TreeOfA[A]) extends TreeOfA[A]

val tree1 = Node(2,Node(1,EmptyBinaryTree,EmptyBinaryTree),
                 Node(3,EmptyBinaryTree,Node(3,
                      EmptyBinaryTree,EmptyBinaryTree)));
```

Exercise 7.2 Given a tree defined using the algebraic data type above, define functions to visit the nodes in preorder and postorder. The output is expected to be a list.

7.3 Data Types and Efficiency Revisited

We have seen in Sect. 6.4 that Scala implements immutable data structures sharing substructures. In this way we do not need to copy all the structure each time we only change part of it. This reduces the time required to update the data structure and the memory needed. To do so, however, Scala needs to provide garbage collection.

Algebraic data types are defined as immutable objects. The way we access and modify them is similar to the way we access and modify lists.

Chapter 8
Parallelism

Scala offers different alternatives for parallelism and multithreading.

The first one is based on threads and synchronization. Scala has a trait `Thread` that we can use to create a thread with a computation to do. This thread requires an object of class `Runnable` (which needs the method `run` implemented). An example that generates two threads of the class `loopToN` is given below. First we implement the class with a method `run` which prints the numbers from 1 to a given value `N`. Objects of this class can be created with `new` and then executed with `run`. Done in this way, we do not have parallelism. The code below creates and runs two instances and we can see on the screen that they are executed sequentially.

```
class loopToN (n: Int) extends Runnable {
  def run() = {
    (1 to n).map((i)=>print(""+i))
  }
}
(new loopToN(10)).run
(new loopToN(10)).run
```

We can create the threads creating a new `Thread` with an instantiation of the class. Then, threads are run with `start`. The execution of the threads print on the screen the numbers from 1 to 100. The two threads created in the code are executed in parallel.

```
val thread1 = new Thread(new loopToN(100))
val thread2 = new Thread(new loopToN(100))
thread1.start; thread2.start
```

© Springer International Publishing AG 2016
V. Torra, *Scala: From a Functional Programming Perspective*, LNCS 9980
DOI: 10.1007/978-3-319-46481-7_8

With multiple threads, Scala offers `synchronized` to avoid different threads accessing the same data.

The second alternative for computing in parallel is based on collections. Scala includes several types of collections that include efficient built-in functions to process them. We discuss them in Sect. 8.1.

The third alternative are actors. Scala offers support for them, which has some advantages over dealing explicitly with threads and synchronization. We present them in Sect. 8.2.

Finally, Scala combines with Spark and can be used for implementing the map-reduce paradigm. We do not discuss this approach here. Note however that the map-reduce paradigm is based on the operations on sequences that we have studied in this book. Recall `map`, `reduceLeft`, and `reduceRight` from Sect. 2.9.4. We will see in Sect. 8.1 still two other higher-order functions: `fold` and `aggregate`.

8.1 Collections

We saw in Sect. 2.9.2 some of the basic collections provided by Scala, including lists, arrays, and ranges. In addition to them, Scala offers some additional collections which have already built-in methods exploiting parallelism.

We can say that the main difference between the two types of collections is that while in the former access to elements is expected in a sequential order (and accessed in a single thread), this is not longer the case for the parallel ones.

The type and classification of parallel collections mimics the one we have already seen. We have both mutable and immutable, and several of the collections have a parallel counterpart. We have e.g. parallel arrays and ranges. We do not have however parallel lists.

The type of parallel collections is prefixed by `Par` and thus, we have `ParArray`, and `ParRange`. To create a parallel collection from a non parallel one we use `par`, and to transform a parallel collection into a standard (non-parallel) one, we use `seq`. For example, we create a parallel array with 5 numbers by `Array(1,2,3,4,5).par`. Similarly, we can transform this parallel sequence into a sequential one by `Array(1,2,3,4,5).par.seq`.

In a way similar to what we did with sequential collections (see again Sect. 2.9.4), we can process all the elements of a parallel sequence using e.g. `foreach`, `map`, `filter`. Recall that `foreach` is used only for its side effects.

To illustrate how we can use them with parallel sequences, and to show that the elements are not processed in order, we give the following code.

```
val resultForEach = Array(1,2,3,4,5).par foreach println
val resultMap = (1 until 10).par.map(
  (i)=>{println(i); String.valueOf(i)})
val resultFilter = (1 until 10).par.filter(
  (i)=>{println(i); i % 3 != 1})
```

If this is typed into the interpreter, we can see (by means of the function with side effects `println`) that elements are not processed in order. For example, the code corresponding to `map` returns (in my execution):

```scala
scala> val resultMap = (1 until 10).par.map(
     |             (i)=>{println(i); String.valueOf(i)})
1
2
3
4
7
8
9
5
6
resultMap: scala.collection.parallel.immutable.ParSeq[String] =
                    ParVector(1, 2, 3, 4, 5, 6, 7, 8, 9)
```

Scala also provides to these parallel structures with the two higher-order functions `foldLeft` and `foldRight`. Nevertheless, they are defined in such a way that the elements are forced to be processed either from the beginning to the end (i.e., the case of `foldLeft`) or from the last to the first (i.e., the case of `foldRight`). The execution of the following code will illustrate this process.

```scala
val resultFoldL = (1 until 10).par.foldLeft("")(
        (a,b)=>{println(b); "("+a+","+b+")"})
val resultFoldR = (1 until 10).par.foldRight("")(
        (a,b)=>{println(a); "("+a+","+b+")"})
```

For example, in the case of `foldRight` we obtain:

```scala
scala> val resultFoldR = (1 until 10).par.foldRight("")(
     |             (a,b)=>{println(a); "("+a+","+b+")"})
9
8
7
6
5
4
3
2
1
resultFoldR: String = (1,(2,(3,(4,(5,(6,(7,(8,(9,)))))))))
```

In order to exploit the fact that the sequence is a parallel one, we can use two alternative functions: `fold` and `aggregate`.

- Fold. It is similar to `foldLeft` and `foldRight` in the sense that combines data and an initial element e_0 by means of a function f. Nevertheless, in `fold`, the order of application of the function is unknown. The sequence is divided into pieces, and then the partial results are combined. Each time we start to process a subsequence we use the element e_0. Then, given a sequence of e.g. 3 elements $< e_1, e_2, e_3 >$

there are different ways to combine them. For example, the following alternatives
are possible:

1. $f(f(e_0, e_1), f(f(e_0, e_2), e_3))$
2. $f(f(f(e_0, e_1), e_2), f(e_0, e_3))$

Because of that, the function f needs the type of all objects involved to be the
same. So, the signature of the function is f: (A, A) => A. Compare this with
the signature of foldLeft in Sect. 2.9.4 (i.e., f: (B, A) => B).
As explained above, fold requires an initial element e_0 to combine. This element
needs to be also of the same type.
We can use this function, for example, to multiply all the elements of a parallel
array as follows.
(1 to 100).par.fold(1)((a,b)=>a*b)
We can use this expression to define a factorial function for any Int as follows.

```
val fact: (Int=>Int) =
  (n) => {(1 to n).par.fold(1)((a,b)=>a*b)}
```

We give another example using fold. The expression is similar to the ones seen
above. It permits to visualize that the order of execution is neither from left to
right, nor from right to left. In addition, each execution may lead to a different
result.

```
val resultFold = (1 until 15).par.fold("0")(
       (a,b)=>{ "("+a+","+b+")" })
```

Two different executions led to the following different results. That is, elements
were combined differently. Observe also the use of the element e_0 (in this case
zero).

```
scala> val resultFold = (1 until 15).par.fold("0")(
     |            (a,b)=>{ "("+a+","+b+")" })
resultFold: Any = ((((0,1),((0,2),(0,3))),(((0,4),(0,5)),
  ((0,6),7))),(((0,8),((0,9),10)),((((0,11),12),13),14)))

scala> val resultFold = (1 until 15).par.fold("0")(
     |            (a,b)=>{ "("+a+","+b+")" })
resultFold: Any = ((((0,1),((0,2),3)),(((0,4),(0,5)),
  ((0,6),7))),(((0,8),((0,9),10)),((((0,11),12),13),14)))
```

- Aggregate. This function is similar to fold, but considering two functions instead
  of one. This is to allow that the type of the elements in the sequence (say A) and
  the type of the output (say B) is different. We have one function that combines
  partial results (say c: (B, B) => B) and another that applies to partial results
  and elements of the initial sequence (say f: (B, A) => B). In addition, we
  have the initial element e_0 of type B. We call aggregate as follows

```
aggregate(e0)(c, f)
```

For example, we can use this function to define a function similar to the previous one. However, in this case the combination of a string and an integer will be done with one function, and the combination of two strings (i.e., combination of partial results) will be done with another one.

```
val resultAggregate = (1 until 15).par.aggregate("_")(
  (a,b) => { "("+a+","+String.valueOf(b)+")" },
  (a,b) => { "["+a+","+b+"]" } )
```

Different applications of this code will lead to different results as the order in which the elements are combined is not determined before hand. We give below the result of two different executions.

```
scala> val resultAggregate = (1 until 15).par.aggregate("_")(
     |     (a,b) => { "("+a+","+String.valueOf(b)+")" },
     |     (a,b) => { "["+a+","+b+"]" } )
resultAggregate: String = [[[(_,1),((_,2),3)],((((_,4),5),6),
7)],[[(_,8),((_,9),10)],((((_,11),12),13),14)]]

scala> val resultAggregate = (1 until 15).par.aggregate("_")(
     |     (a,b) => { "("+a+","+String.valueOf(b)+")" },
     |     (a,b) => { "["+a+","+b+"]" } )
resultAggregate: String = [[[(_,1),((_,2),3)],[[(_,4),(_,5)],
((_,6),7)]],[[(_,8),((_,9),10)],((((_,11),12),13),14)]]
```

8.2 Actors

The most important model for parallelism in Scala are actors. Actors have their origin in a paper by C. Hewitt et al. [7] in 1973. We can see this model as a higher-level model, avoiding to deal explicitly with threads and synchronization. This model is well integrated into the object-oriented paradigm, and can be used to implement multi-agent systems [20] (in the context of artificial intelligence).

Actors help to develop software with less errors. As [6] points out, the difference is between shared-state concurrency and message passing. In the former we can have data races (i.e., when different concurrent threads access and modify the same data) which can cause errors. This is avoided with message passing at the cost of a higher communication overhead. In actors, we have that variables are (or are expected to be) local.

This section gives a short overview of actors in Scala. For a more detailed description we refer the reader to [6]. This reference also includes a discussion on the advantages and inconveniences of this model in contrast to shared-state concurrency. Actors in the context of object-oriented programming are discussed in detail in [11] (a book that was written well before Scala was defined).

8.2.1 Definition

Actors can be seen as objects that are executed independently, that have their own variables and knowledge, and that communicate between each other with message passing.

It is important to remark that in this model, message passing is the only way to communicate, and that all variables are local to the actors. Actors will send messages to other actors and will react to messages they receive. We describe below how actors are defined in Scala. We will also give an example of their use to illustrate the description.

The example implements a supermarket. The supermarket has several people that has selected a list of products and wants to pay them, and a cashier that informs about the price of each selected product and receives the payment. The implementation assumes that all people behave in a correct way and that we can trust the people to do the addition of their products.

We will implement the supermarket having two types of actors. One for the cashier and the other for the customers. Then, we assume that there is a single cashier but we can have as many customers as required.

Let us consider now the different components that define a program with actors. We start defining the messages to be transmitted. Then, we explain how to define actors, and discuss the implementation of the method `act` that is the one that implements actors' behavior.

- **Definition of the messages.** Messages are defined by means of case classes. Because of that we need to distinguish between messages with parameters and those without. The former will be defined by means of case objects and the latter by means of case classes.

In our example, we will consider different types of messages. We will have three messages that corresponds to three types of products. These messages will be used by the customers to inform the cashier about what they have selected. We have considered the products `Newspaper`, `Chocolates`, and `Cheese`. We define all of them as extensions of `Product`. We consider `Newspaper` as a non-parametric product and the other as parametric. For `Chocolates` we include the grams bought (a `Double`), and for `Cheese` the type of the cheese (a `String`) and the grams bought (also a `Double`).

We will have three additional messages. The customer will send information of the product to the cashier, and the cashier will respond with the price. This is therefore a message with a parameter of type `Double`. The name of the message is `Price`. Then, once the price of all products are known, the customer will send to the cashier a message with the total to be paid. This message, with name `Total` has also a parameter that is of type `Double`. To finish the transaction we have a message `Thanks` with no parameter.

So, as a summary, we have two messages with no parameters and four with parameters. The declaration we need to do is the following one.

```
private case object Newspaper extends Product
private case object Thanks
private case class Total (p: Double)
private case class Chocolates (grams:
  Double) extends Product
private case class Cheese (t: String,
  grams: Double) extends Product
private case class Price (euros: Double)
```

- **Definition of each actor.** Actors are defined in terms of a class that extends the `actors.Actor` class. Importing `actors._` we can simplify the notation.

```
import actors._
class ourActor extends Actor {
  // code for our actor
}
```

- **Implementation of the method act.** Each actor requires a method `act` that implements the behavior of the actor. A typical structure for this method is to `loop` forever and only react when messages are received (using `receive`). `loop` is provided for this purpose. Therefore, the method act may have a structure as the following one.

```
def act () = {
  loop {
    receive {
      case ...
    }
  }
}
```

In our example we will implement two type of actors. One is the class `Cashier` and the other is the class `Customer`. Both classes will extend `actors.Actor`. They will implement the method `act`.

Both classes have parameters. The `Cashier` has a `Double` corresponding to the initial amount of money (i.e., variable `Cash`) the `Cashier` has. The `Customer` has three parameters, one is the list of products to be bought (or paid), the second one is the name of this customer. We use names to print them on the screen in order to track what customers are doing. The third parameter is the actor to whom the customer sends the messages. When we instantiate the class `customer` to create particular customers, all will receive the same cashier as argument.

```
class Cashier (private[this] var cash: Double)
                                        extends Actor {
  def act () = {
    println ("Cashier")
    //
  }
```

```
  }
class Customer (private[this] var products: List[Product],
  cashier: Actor, var name: String)
extends Actor {
  def act () = {
    println ("Customer's name:"+name)
    // missing code
  }
}
```

– **Sending messages.** Messages are sent with the notation

```
message-receiver ! message
```

Here, `message-receiver` should be the name of an actor. This can be an explicit name, but it can also be `sender`. `sender` is a method of the class `Actor` that returns the actor that sent the last received message. For example, when the `cashier` receives a message `Total` with the total amount received, we will reply with

```
sender ! Thanks
```

and the customer will send to the cashier a message for each of the products to be paid with (recall that `cashier` is a variable of the class that denotes an Actor) the following line of code

```
products.map((x) => cashier ! x)
```

We have seen that we can send messages with `!`. However, this is not the only way to send messages. We can also use `!?` which is for synchronous messages. That is, the thread is blocked until the message is sent and a reply is received. We will give an example below using `!?` in Sect. 8.2.2. A third alternative is `!!` which corresponds to `futures`. They can be used to launch computations that return a (future) result, and then when we need the value, if the value is still not available, the thread is blocked until it is available.

When we want to send a message as a reply to a message we have received, we can also use the method `reply`. This method has a parameter that is the message to be transmitted.

We will give below (see Sect. 8.2.3) an example using futures. The example also uses `reply`. We will have an actor that launches a future with name `future` and then prints its result. This is done printing the value `future()` (as the future is a function). The other actor sends its result (the value to be printed) with `reply`.

– **Receiving messages.** We can express that we are waiting for messages to be replied with `receive`. We will then consider a set of cases for each type of message. We use pattern matching with `case` to distinguish the cases.

In our example, the `cashier` is waiting for messages about products (i.e., `Newspaper`, `Chocolates`, and `Cheese`) and about the total (i.e., the message `Total`). So, there are four cases. Each type of message is considered separately. For the three products we compute their price (that may depend on the type and the weight) and send the price to the sender. For the total, we accumulate the amount to the cashiers' cash and reply the sender with Thanks. The code includes some println that provide lateral effects in order to visualize how data is processed.

```
receive {
  case Total (p) => {
    cash = cash + p
    println ("Cashier.Thanks. Total cash:"+cash)
    sender ! Thanks }
  case Newspaper => {
    println ("Cashier.Newspaper");
    sender ! Price (2.5) }
  case Chocolates (grams) => {
    println ("Cashier.Chocolate");
    sender ! Price ( grams * 0.015) }
  case Cheese (t, grams) => {
    println ("Cashier.Cheese");
    if (t=="Camembert") {
      sender ! Price ( grams * 0.01 ) }
    else { sender ! Price ( grams * 0.02 ) }
  }
}
```

Each customer receives the prices of all the products bought. This is implemented by means of a loop that is repeated as many times as the number of products, and each time we receive a message of type Price. The amounts received are accumulated in the variable total.

```
while (toReceive!=0) {
  receive {
    case Price (euros) => {
      println (name+".Price:"+euros);
      total = total + euros
      toReceive = toReceive-1
    }
  }
}
```

When all prices are received, the customer sends the total to the cashier, and waits until the cashier sends a Thanks. This means that customer has completed the payment. We include below this part of code.

```
cashier ! Total(total);
receive {
  case Thanks => { println (name+".finish") }
```

– **Instantiation and execution of the actors.** Once the classes are created, we need to instantiate the actors and start them. We can instantiate the actors with

new (as we do with classes) with appropriate parameters. Then, we start them
by applying `start` to the actor.

In our example, we put all these definitions in the object `supermarket`,
which includes a method called `run` that instantiates a `cashier` and two
`customers`. The method also starts these actors. The code includes also some
printing messages to inform that the calls have been done. The code follows.

```
def run () = {
  println("supermarket")
  val cashier = new Cashier(0)
  val customer1 = new Customer(
    List(Newspaper,Newspaper,Newspaper),
    "Customer-1", cashier)
  val customer2 = new Customer(
    List(Newspaper,Chocolates(1000),
         Cheese("Cabrales",1000)),
    "Customer-2", cashier)
  cashier.start
  println("cashier started")
  customer1.start
  println("customer-1 started")
  customer2.start
  println("customer-2 started")
}
```

We give the complete code of this example below. If we execute the example (run-
ning `supermarket.run`) we will see in the screen what is printed with `println`.
You will notice that different executions will lead to the appearance of the messages
in (slightly) different order. While there are some constraints in our program (e.g.,
`Thanks` follows the `Total` payment, and this follows the correct reception of all
messages corresponding to all products of a customer), there is some freedom in the
order of the other messages.

```
object supermarket {
  import actors._

  private case object Newspaper extends Product
  private case object Thanks
  private case class Total (p: Double)
  private case class Chocolates (grams: Double) extends Product
  private case class Cheese (t: String,
    grams: Double) extends Product
  private case class Price (euros: Double)

  class Cashier (private[this] var cash: Double) extends Actor {
    def act () = {
      println ("Cashier")
      loop {
        receive {
          case Total (p) => {
            cash = cash + p
            println ("Cashier.Thanks. Total cash:"+cash)
```

```
                  sender ! Thanks }
            case Newspaper => {
              println ("Cashier.Newspaper"); sender ! Price (2.5) }
            case Chocolates (grams) => {
              println ("Cashier.Chocolate");
              sender ! Price ( grams * 0.015) }
            case Cheese (t, grams) => {
              println ("Cashier.Cheese");
              if (t=="Camembert") { sender ! Price ( grams * 0.01 ) }
              else { sender ! Price ( grams * 0.02 ) }
            }
        }
      }
   }
}
class Customer (private[this] var products: List[Product],
   var name: String,
   cashier: Actor)
extends Actor {
   def act () = {
     println ("Customer's name:"+name)
     var total: Double = 0
     var toReceive = products.length
     products.map((x) => cashier ! x)
     while (toReceive!=0) {
       receive {
         case Price (euros) => {
           println (name+".Price:"+euros);
           total = total + euros
           toReceive = toReceive-1
         }
       }
     }
     println (name+".pay total:"+total)
     cashier ! Total(total);
     receive {
       case Thanks => { println (name+".finish") }
     }
   }
}
def run () = {
   println("supermarket")
   val cashier = new Cashier(0)
   val customer1 = new Customer(List(Newspaper,Newspaper,Newspaper),
             "Customer-1", cashier)
   val customer2 = new Customer(List(Newspaper,Chocolates(1000),
                                     Cheese("Cabrales",1000)),
             "Customer-2", cashier)
   cashier.start
   println("cashier started")
   customer1.start
   println("customer-1 started")
   customer2.start
   println("customer-2 started")
 }
}
```

8.2.2 Receive and React, ! and !?

We have explained that we can use `receive` to force the actor to listen and deal with messages. With `receive` the thread that runs the actor is blocked until a message arrives.

An alternative to `receive` is `react`, which does not block the thread. In fact, the event handler is launched (to wait the arrival of messages) and then the thread is released. This implies that the code following a `react` will never be executed, and, thus, `react` is the last thing an actor has to do. We cannot use `react` within a `while`, but within a `loop` it works as expected (i.e., several messages are processed). We say that actors with `react` are event-based as all their actions are caused by events. The others are thread-based. The new Scala actor model (the Akka's actor model) is event-based.

So, in the example, if we replace `receive` by `react` in the `Cashier` the program of the supermarked will work correctly. Nevertheless, if we make the same replacement in the first `react` of the `Customer` the program does not work correctly. This is so because the event handler for `case Price (euros)` will be launched, but when this message arrives, the code of this handler is executed (i.e., we see in the screen `Customer-1.Price:2.5`) but only one of these messages is handled and the remaining part of the code is never executed. In order to wait for all prices, we can define a recursive function to deal with the appropriate number of prices (i.e., `toReceive`) and calls itself within the react. So, when the message is handled, the last thing to be done is to call the function again. The function accumulates all the prices and when there is no other message to wait, it sends the total to the `cashier`. The new implementation of `Customer` given below follows this approach.

As we have stated above, we can use `!?` to send messages in a synchronous way. That is, when the message is sent, the thread is blocked until is read and replied. In our revised version of the example, we will use `!?` when the `customer` sends the `Total` to the `cashier`. Then, we block the thread until the `cashier` replies. As this synchronous way of sending returns the reply, in our code we assign this reply to the variable `reply`. Then, we can use it to distinguish about possible replies by means of a `match` with the alternative cases. In this particular example, there is only one possible reply, which is `Thanks`. These particular lines of code are as follows:

```
val reply = cashier !? Total(total)
reply match {
  case Thanks => println(name+"received thanks")
}
```

The full code of the actor `Customer` with the two major changes described above follows.

```
class Customer (private[this] var products: List[Product],
  var name: String,
  cashier: Actor)
extends actors.Actor {
  def allPrices (toReceive: Int, total: Double):Unit = {
    if (toReceive==0) {
      println (name+".pay total:"+total)
      val reply = cashier !? Total(total)
      reply match {
        case Thanks => println(name+"received thanks")
```

```
            }
          }
        else {
          react {
            case Price (euros) => {
              println (name+".Price:"+euros)
              allPrices(toReceive-1, total + euros)
            }
          }
        }
      }
    }
  def act () = {
    println ("Customer's name:"+name)
    var total: Double = 0
    var toReceive = products.length
    products.map((x) => cashier ! x)
    allPrices (toReceive, total)
    receive {
      case Thanks => { println (name+".finish") }
    }
  }
}
```

8.2.3 Futures and !!

In this section we revise the last version of the implementation of supermarket using futures. We will use the future for the Total (after all prices are already obtained). Using a future we expect that the cashier will give us a result, which is stored in a variable. We call this variable future. After creating this future, the actor can do any other computation and then, when the value of the future is needed we access it with future(). In our case, we just print the value. So, the code for the customer is as follows see Sect. 8.2.5:

```
val future = cashier !! Total(total)
// do other computations
println("Future:"+future())
```

In order for the program to work properly, we need that the customer sends the result of the future when the message Total is processed. In our simple example we just reply with a string. This is done with the following code for the cashier

```
case Total (p) => {
  cash = cash + p
  println ("Cashier.Thanks. Total cash:"+cash)
  reply("Cashier replies thanks!!") }
```

We give below the full code of this version of supermarket with futures.

```
// Version with futures
object supermarket {
  import actors._
  private case object Newspaper extends Product
  private case object Thanks
  private case class Total (p: Double)
  private case class Chocolates (grams: Double) extends Product
  private case class Cheese (t: String,
    grams: Double) extends Product
  private case class Price (euros: Double)

  class Cashier (private[this] var cash: Double) extends Actor {
    def act () = {
      println ("Cashier")
      loop {
      react {
        case Total (p) => {
          cash = cash + p
          println ("Cashier.Thanks. Total cash:"+cash)
          reply("Cashier replies thanks!!") }
        case Newspaper => {
          println ("Cashier.Newspaper"); sender ! Price (2.5) }
        case Chocolates (grams) => {
          println ("Cashier.Chocolate");
          sender ! Price ( grams * 0.015) }
          case Cheese (t, grams) => {
            println ("Cashier.Cheese");
            if (t=="Camembert") { sender ! Price ( grams * 0.01 ) }
            else { sender ! Price ( grams * 0.02 ) }
          }
      }}
      println ("Cashier. Code after react")
    }
  }
  class Customer (private[this] var products: List[Product],
    var name: String,
    cashier: Actor)
  extends actors.Actor {
    def allPrices (toReceive: Int, total: Double):Unit = {
      if (toReceive==0) {
        println (name+".pay total:"+total)
        val future = cashier !! Total(total)
        // do other computations
        println("Future:"+future())
      }
      else {
        react {
          case Price (euros) => {
            println (name+".Price:"+euros)
            allPrices(toReceive-1, total + euros)
          }
        }
      }
    }
    def act () = {
      println ("Customer's name:"+name)
      var total: Double = 0
      var toReceive = products.length
      products.map((x) => cashier ! x)
      allPrices (toReceive, total)
      receive {
        case Thanks => { println (name+".finish") }
      }
    }
  }
```

```
def run () = {
  println("supermarket")
  val cashier = new Cashier(0)
  val customer1 = new Customer(
    List(Newspaper,Newspaper,Newspaper),
    "Customer-1", cashier)
  val customer2 = new Customer(
    List(Newspaper,Chocolates(1000),
         Cheese("Cabrales",1000)),
    "Customer-2", cashier)
  cashier.start
  println("cashier started")
  customer1.start
  println("customer-1 started")
  customer2.start
  println("customer-2 started")
  println("customer2.getState="+customer2.getState)
  }
}
```

8.2.4 Others

There are other control structures and methods for implementing actors. For example, they include `exit` to terminate the execution of an actor, and the method `getState` that when applied to an actor informs of its state. E.g., we can call `customer2.getState`.

8.2.5 Akka's Actor Model

From Scala 2.10.0 the default actor library is Akka. It follows an event-based approach. There are differences between both actor models. We illustrate the definition of the actors in Akka revisiting the example of the supermarket.

Actors require a main method `receive` to process all incoming messages. In addition, if we need some initializations, we implement the method `preStart` and if we need to do some work when the actor is terminated we implement `postStop`. The methods `preStart` and `postStop` will be defined with `override` as there are default versions.

In our example, the actor Customer will have a `preStart` method that will send all the messages with all the products bought. In contrast, the cashier only contains the method `receive`. Variables to be used by the actor (and these methods) will be defined as local to the actor.

The method receive consists on a set of cases, one for each message, describing how to proceed with each one. We do not need to loop here. In this event-based approach, we have a reactive actor that just reacts to arriving messages.

For sending messages, we have two options in Akka. The first one `!` sends a message asynchronously and is equivalent to `!` in the other actor model. The second option is `?` that also sends a message asynchronously but in this case it returns a future. In this case, if we want to wait the result of this future we need to make explicit this waiting (with `result`) and we need to supply a timout. `result` belongs to the object `Await`. This object includes also a method `ready`. `?` is in package `akka.pattern.ask`.

In our example, we use `Await.result` to implement the `Customer` as we decided to use a future when sending the message `Total`.

Due to the fact that the actor is event-based, and there is only a single method `receive` to deal all messages, the implementation is slightly different from the one given in the previous sections. In this case the actor will process any message at any time, including `Thanks`. Nevertheless, `Thanks` will only terminate the actor when all `Prices` have been received.

The Akka actor system is started with `ActorSystem` and actors are created with `actorOf` with `Props`. `Props` is to specify the options for creating actors, including the arguments of the actors. In our case, we have parameters in the two type of actors. We can terminate an actor with `context.stop(self)`.

The code of the agents using Akka follows. We can execute this code using `supermarket.run` (as before).

```
object supermarket {
  import akka.actor._
  import akka.pattern.ask
  import akka.util._
  import scala.concurrent.duration._
  import scala.concurrent.Await
  private case object Newspaper extends Product
  private case object Thanks
  private case class Total (p: Double)
  private case class Chocolates (grams: Double) extends Product
  private case class Cheese (t: String, grams: Double) extends Product
  private case class Price (euros: Double)
  class Cashier (private[this] var cash: Double) extends Actor {
    def receive = {
      case Total (p) => {
        cash = cash + p
        println ("Cashier.Thanks. Total cash:"+cash)
        sender ! "Cashier replies thanks!!" }
      case Newspaper => {
        println ("Cashier.Newspaper"); sender ! Price (2.5) }
      case Chocolates (grams) => {
        println ("Cashier.Chocolate");
        sender ! Price ( grams * 0.015) }
      case Cheese (t, grams) => {
        println ("Cashier.Cheese");
        if (t=="Camembert") { sender ! Price ( grams * 0.01 ) }
        else { sender ! Price ( grams * 0.02 ) }
      }
    }
  }
  class Customer (private[this] var products: List[Product],
    var name: String,
    cashier: ActorRef)
  extends Actor {
    private var total: Double = 0
    private var toReceive = products.length
    override def preStart():Unit = {
      println ("Customer's name:"+name)
      products.map((x) => cashier ! x)
    }
    def receive = {
```

```
        case Price (euros) => {
          println (name+".Price:"+euros)
          toReceive = toReceive-1
          total = total + euros
          if (toReceive==0) {
            println (name+".pay total:"+total)
            implicit val timeout = Timeout(5 seconds)
            val future = cashier ? Total(total)
            // do other computations
            val result = Await.result(future,
                           timeout.duration).asInstanceOf[String]
            println("Future:"+result)
            }
          }
        case Thanks => {
          if (toReceive==0) {
            println (name+".finish"); context.stop(self) }
          else { println (name+".not yet finished"); }
          }
        case _ => { println ("Other messages"); }
      }
    }
  def run () = {
    println("supermarket")
    val system = ActorSystem("Supermarket")
    val cashier = system.actorOf(Props(new Cashier(0)),
                                    name="Cashier")
    val customer1 = system.actorOf(Props(new Customer(
      List(Newspaper,Newspaper,Newspaper), "Customer-1", cashier)))
    val customer2 = system.actorOf(Props(new Customer(
      List(Newspaper,Chocolates(1000),Cheese("Cabrales",1000)),
      "Customer-2", cashier)))
  }
}
```

Chapter 9
Solutions

Problems of Chapter 2

2.1 The following solution solves the problem, but only for the cases that the solutions are real. I.e., the case that the discriminant is zero or positive. In Sect. 4.7 we give another definition with complex numbers.

```
(a: Double, b: Double, c: Double) => {
  val d = b*b-4*a*c
      ((-b - Math.sqrt(d))/(2*a),
       (-b + Math.sqrt(d))/(2*a))
}
```

To find the solution of $x^2 - 3 = 0$ we would apply the function as follows.

```
((a: Double, b: Double, c: Double) => {
  val d = b*b-4*a*c
      ((-b - Math.sqrt(d))/(2*a),
       (-b + Math.sqrt(d))/(2*a))
})(1,0,-3)
```

2.2 The function to compute the Fibonacci series is given below. We can use it to compute F_5 with fib(5).

```
val fib: (Int=>Int) = (n) => {
  if (n==0) { 1 }
  else if (n==1) { 1 }
  else { fib(n-1) + fib(n-2) }
}
```

The function to solve the problem of the towers of Hanoi is given below. We use a String to denote the pegs. We can call the function using hanoi(2,"Peg Origin", "Peg Final", "Peg Other").

© Springer International Publishing AG 2016
V. Torra, *Scala: From a Functional Programming Perspective*, LNCS 9980
DOI: 10.1007/978-3-319-46481-7_9

```scala
val hanoi: ((Int, String, String, String)=>Unit) =
      (n, origin, dest, using) => {
  if (n==1) {
    println("Move disk"+1+"from"+origin+"to"+dest)}
  else if (n > 1) {
    hanoi(n-1,origin,using,dest)
    println("Move disk"+n+"from"+origin+"to"+dest)
    hanoi(n-1,using,dest,origin)
    }
}
```

2.4 We give two solutions. The first one is recursive but not using pattern matching and the second uses pattern mathing.

```scala
// Recursive version
val from: ((Int,Int) => List[Int]) = (n,m) => {
  if (n==m) { List(m) }
  else n::from(n+1,m)
}
// Recursive version using pattern matching
val from: ((Int,Int) => List[Int]) = (n,m) => {
  (n-m) match {
    case 0 => List(n)
    case _ => (n)::from(n+1,m)
  }
}
```

Note also that the following solution using pattern matching does not work. Scala considers m within the match as a new variable and then n can always be matched with this (new) m. Scala gives a warning, informing that the following line _ is unreachable (which is true) but does not inform that there is another variable m in the function.

```scala
val from: ((Int,Int) => List[Int]) = (n,m) => {
  n match {
    case m => List(n)
    case _ => (n)::from(n+1,m)
  }
}
```

2.5 We can solve quicksort as follows.

```scala
val quicksort: (List[Int]=>List[Int]) = (l) => {
  l match {
    case Nil => Nil
    case hd::tl => quicksort(tl.filter(_<=hd)) ::: hd ::
                   quicksort(tl.filter(_>hd))
  }
}
```

We can call it using

```
quicksort(List(5,6,8,3,2,5,6))
```

2.6 We can define `curryF` as follows.

```
val curryF:(Double => (Double => (Double => Double))) =
  (a) => {
    (b) => {
      (c) => {
        a*(b+c)*(b+c)
}}}
```

This definition works properly with the following two calls

```
curryF (2)(3)(1)
List(1.0,2.0,3.0).map(curryF(2)(3))
```

2.7 A function to add only the positive elements of a list can be defined as follows.

```
val sumPos: (List[Int]=>Int) = (1) => {
    1.filter(n=>(n>0)).foldLeft(0)((a,b)=>a+b)  }
sumPos(List(1,-2,5,-3))
```

2.8 The solution of the internal product is as follows.

```
val prod:(((Int,Int))=>Int) =
  (a) => a match { case (a1,a2) => a1*a2 }
    ((1 to 5).zip(0 to 4).map(prod)).foldLeft(0)((a,b)=>a+b)
val intProd:((List[Int],List[Int])=>Int) = (vec1,vec2) => {
  (vec1.zip(vec2).map(prod)).foldLeft(0)((a,b)=>a+b)  }
intProd(List(1,2,3,4,5),List(0,1,2,3,4))
```

Problems of Chapter 3

3.1 The solution of this exercise is similar to the function `lazyConditional`

```
val switch:((Int, => Int, => Int, => Int) => Int) =
   (x,case1,case2,case3) => {
  x match {
    case 1 => case1
    case 2 => case2
    case 3 => case3
  }
}
```

We can test this function with

```
switch(1,100,200/0,300/0)
switch(2,100,200,300)
```

3.2 We can print the numbers using the `for` construction as

```
for (i <- naturalNumbers)  println(i)
```

However, as the stream is infinite, the system will give an error and can crash after printing a large set of numbers. In a similar way, we can apply the function `last` to a stream, and, naturally, also to `naturalNumbers`. Nevertheless, as the stream is infinite this will also cause an error and, eventually, a system crash.

3.3 We can solve this problem as follows.

```
val evenFilter = nats.filter((a) => a % 2 == 0)
val oddFilter = nats.filter((a) => a % 2 != 0)
```

3.4 We give two solutions of this problem. One with a local definition, and the other using map.

```
val newRow: (List[Int] => List[Int]) = (row) => {
  lazy val newRowR: (List[Int] => List[Int]) =
    (row) => row match {
      case Nil => List(1)
      case hd::Nil => 1::Nil
      case hd::tl => hd+tl.head::newRowR(tl)
    }
  1::newRowR(row)
}
val newRow: (List[Int] => List[Int]) = (row) => {
  1::row.zip(row.tail:::List.(0)).map((a)=>(a._1+a._2))
}
```

We can call `newRow` as follows:

```
newRow(List(1))
newRow(List(1,4,6,4,1))
```

The second part can be solved as follows.

```
val buildAllRows: (List[Int] => Stream[List[Int]]) =
  (l) => l #:: buildAllRows(newRow(l))
val allPascal = buildAllRows(List(1))
```

3.6 We give the solution of the three functions of the exercise. They are the functions qn, dr, and dn below.

```
val nats: (Stream[Int]) = 1#:: (nats.map((a)=>a+1))
val qn: (Stream[Int]) = {
  1#::1#::
  ((nats.tail).zip(qn.tail)).map((a)=>a._1-a._2).map(
    (a)=>qn(a)).zip(((nats.tail).zip(qn)).map(
    (a)=>a._1-a._2).map((a)=>qn(a))).map((a)=>a._1+a._2)
}
\\ to test:
qn.take(10) foreach println
```

```
val dr: (Int => Int) = (n) => {
  if (n==1) { 1 }
  else {if (n==2) { 1 }
    else { dr(dr(n-1))+dr(n-1-dr(n-2)) }
  }
}
// to test:
dr(4)

val nats: (Stream[Int]) = 1#:: (nats.map((a)=>a+1))
val dn: (Stream[Int]) = {
  0#::1#::1#::
  (dn.tail.tail).map(
    (a)=>dn(a)).zip(((nats.tail).zip(dn.tail)).map(
      (a)=>a._1-a._2).map((a)=>dn(a))).map((a)=>a._1+a._2)
}
// to test:
dn.take(10) foreach println
```

3.7 We define the function `interleave` as follows.

```
val interleave: (Stream[Int],Stream[Int])=>Stream[Int] =
  (s1,s2) => {
    s1.head#::s2.head#::interleave(s1.tail,s2.tail) }
```

3.8

```
val nats: (Stream[Int]) = 1#:: (nats.map((a)=>a+1))
val r = new scala.util.Random()
val seqSin = nats.map((n)=>Math.sin(n*1.0/2))
val seqSinE =
  nats.map((n)=>Math.sin(n*1.0/2)+0.1*r.nextDouble())
```

To visualize some elements of the list we can call the following function

```
seqSinE.take(10) foreach println
```

3.9 We divide the solution into three parts. The first part is the moving average of order 3.

```
// From pair-pair ((a,b),c) to 3-tuple
def fromPPto3T[A](pp: ((A,A),A)) =
  (pp._1._1, pp._1._2, pp._2)

val ma: (Stream[Double] => Stream[Double]) = (x) => {
  x(0)#::(x zip x.tail zip x.tail.tail).map(fromPPto3T).map(
    (a)=>((a._1+a._2+a._3)/3.0))
}
```

We can test this function with

```
ma(seqSinE).take(10) foreach println
```

The second part is the weighted moving average of order 5.

```
// From pair-of-pairs ((((a,b),c),d),e) to List of 5 elements
def fromPofPtoList[A](pp: ((((A,A),A),A),A)) = List(
  pp._1._1._1._1, pp._1._1._1._2,
  pp._1._1._2, pp._1._2, pp._2)

// currified internal product of two vectors \sum_i w_i x_i
def ip(w: List[Double]): List[Double] => Double = (x) => {
  w.zip(x).map((a)=>a._1*a._2).foldLeft(0.0)((a,b) => a+b)}
// Test with: ip(List(0.1,0.2))(List(10,5))

val wa: (List[Double] => (Stream[Double] => Stream[Double])) =
  (w) => {
  (x) => {
  x(0)#::x(1)#::
    (x zip x.tail
     zip x.tail.tail zip x.tail.tail.tail zip
      x.tail.tail.tail.tail).map(fromPofPtoList).map(ip(w))
  }
}
```

We can test this function with

```
wa(List(0.2,0.2,0.2,0.2,0.2))
wa(List(0.2,0.2,0.2,0.2,0.2))(seqSinE)
wa(List(1.0/14,2.0/14,4.0/7,2.0/14,1.0/14))
wa(List(1.0/14,2.0/14,4.0/7,2.0/14,1.0/14))(seqSinE)
```

The third part is the comparison between two sequences. We substract them and then compute the maximum difference between the first n terms.

```
def subst(s1:Stream[Double],
  s2:Stream[Double]): Stream[Double] = {
    s1.zip(s2).map((a)=>a._1-a._2)
}

val difSeqWA = subst(seqSin,
  wa(List(1.0/14,2.0/14,4.0/7,2.0/14,1.0/14))(seqSinE))
val difSeqSE = subst(seqSin,seqSinE)

difSeqSE.take(100).foldLeft(100.0)(Math.min)
difSeqWA.take(100).foldLeft(100.0)(Math.min)
```

Problems of Chapter 4

4.1 To solve this problem we redefine the method dist0 using override.

```
class Complex (override val re: Double, val im: Double) extends
  Real (re) {
    def this (r: Double) = this(r, 0)
```

```
      override def toString = "c"+re.toString+"+"+im.toString
      def +(c2: Complex): Complex =
        new Complex (re + c2.re, im + c2.im)
      def -(c2: Complex): Complex =
        new Complex (re - c2.re, im - c2.im)
      override def dist0: Real = new Real (Math.sqrt(re*re+im*im))
}
```

Problems of Chapter 5

5.1 We give the definition and examples of their use.

```
def from[A] (vFrom:A,vTo:A,gen:A=>A):List[A] = {
  if (vFrom==vTo) { List(vTo) }
  else vFrom::from(gen(vFrom),vTo,gen)
}
from(3,10,(n:Int)=>(n+1))
from(2,10,(n:Int)=>(n+2))
from("a","k",(s:String)=>(s.head + 1).toChar.toString)
from(16,256,(n:Int)=>(n*2))
```

5.2 We can define quicksort for arbitrary types and a function lt on these types as follows

```
def quicksort[A] (l:List[A],lt:(A,A)=>Boolean):List[A] = {
  l match {
    case Nil => Nil
    case hd::tl =>
      quicksort(tl.filter((e)=>(lt(e,hd))),lt) ::: hd ::
      quicksort(tl.filter((e)=>(!(lt(e,hd)))),lt)
  }
}
```

We can test this function with:

```
quicksort[Int](List(5,6,8,3,2,5,6),(a:Int,b:Int)=>(a<b))
quicksort(List(5,6,8,3,2,5,6),(a:Int,b:Int)=>(a<b))
```

Problems of Chapter 6

6.1 We will use the solution of Exercise 2.2 for the tail recursive version of the Fibonacci and the code in this chapter for the straightforward solution. That is,

```
val fibTR:(Int=>Int) = (n) => {
  def fibtr (n:Int, f1:Int, f2:Int):Int = {
    if (n==0) { f1 }
    else { fibtr (n-1, f2, f1+f2) }}
  fibtr(n,0,1)
}

val fibSR: (Int=>Int) = (n) => {
  if (n==0) { 1 }
  else if (n==1) { 1 }
  else { fib(n-1) + fib(n-2) }
}
```

Mean execution times can be computed then as follows.

```
meanET(1000,fibTR(40))
meanET(1000,fibSR(40))
```

References

1. Aho, A.V., Ullman, J.D., Hopcroft, J.E.: Data Structures and Algorithms. Pearson (1983)
2. Backus, J.: Can programming be liberated from the von Neumann Style? A functional style and its algebra of programs. Commun. ACM **21**(8), 613–641 (1978)
3. Chiusano, P., Bjarnason, R.: Functional Programming in Scala. Manning Publications, New York (2015)
4. Cormen, T.H., Leiserson, C.E., Rivest, R.L., Stein, C.: Introduction to Algorithms. The MIT Press, Cambridge (2001)
5. Dijkstra, E.W.: A review of the 1977 Turing Award lecture by John Backus (1979). https://www.cs.utexas.edu/users/EWD/ewd06xx/EWD692.PDF
6. Haller, P., Sommers, F.: Actors in Scala. Artima Press, Walnut Creek (2011)
7. Hewitt, C., Bishop, P., Steiger, R.: A universal modular actor formalism for artificial intelligence. In: Proceedings of IJCAI (1973)
8. Hunt, J.: A Beginner's Guide to Scala, Object Orientation and Functional Programming. Springer, Switzerland (2014)
9. Lewis, M.C.: Introduction to the Art of Programming Using Scala. CRC Press, Boca Raton (2013)
10. Mac Lane, S.: Categories for the Working Mathematician. Springer, New York (1991)
11. Masini, G., Napoli, A., Colnet, D., Léonard, D., Tombre, K.: Les langages à objets. InterEditions, Paris (1989). 2nd edn. (1997)
12. McCarthy, J.: Recursive functions of symbolic expressions and their computation by machine. Part I. Commun. ACM **3**(4), 184–195 (1960)
13. McCarthy, J.: History of LISP. In: Wexelblat, R.L. History of Programming Languages. Academic Press, New York (1981). http://www-formal.stanford.edu/jmc/history/lisp.ps
14. Rosen, K.H.: Discrete Mathematics and Its Applications, 7th edn. McGraw Hill, Boston (2012)
15. Scott, M.L.: Programming Language Pragmatics. Elsevier, Amsterdam (2011)
16. Seldin, J.P.: The logic of Curry and Church. In: Handbook of the History of Logic, vol. 5, pp. 819–874. North-Holland (2006)
17. Smith, G.C.: Algebra and Analysis. Springer, London (1998)
18. Torra, V., Narukawa, Y.: Modeling Decisions: Information Fusion and Aggregation Operators. Springer, New York (2007)
19. Watt, D.A.: Programming Language Concepts and Paradigms. Prentice Hall, New York (1990)
20. Wooldridge, M.: An Introduction to Multiagent Systems. Wiley, New York (2002)

URLs and Web pages

21. http://docs.scala-lang.org/glossary/
22. http://docs.scala-lang.org/overviews/collections/creating-collections-from-scratch.html
23. http://docs.scala-lang.org/style/files.html
24. http://docs.scala-lang.org/tutorials/tour/anonymous-function-syntax.html
25. http://www.scala-lang.org/old/node/111
26. https://jupyter.org/index.html
27. http://scala-ide.org/
28. http://stackoverflow.com/questions/8316406/get-superclasses-function-in-scala
29. http://cstheory.stackexchange.com/questions/625/relationship-between-turing-machine-and-lambda-calculus

Index

© Springer International Publishing AG 2016
V. Torra, *Scala: From a Functional Programming Perspective*, LNCS 9980
DOI: 10.1007/978-3-319-46481-7

Printed in the United States
By Bookmasters